Portage. April 17. 1825

CREDITS

EDITOR Barbara Huck

ASSOCIATE EDITOR Peter St. John

PHOTOGRAPHY Dennis Fast, Ann Love, Andrew Marshall, Liz Saul, Peter St. John, Joel Walker, Barry Wallace

DESIGN & MAPS Dawn Huck

IMAGE RESEARCH & PERMISSIONS EDITOR Jane Huck

PREPRESS & PRINTING Friesens, Manitoba

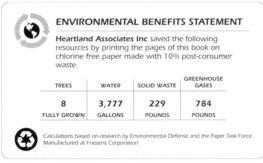

ENVIRONMENTAL BENEFITS STATEMENT

Heartland Associates Inc saved the following resources by printing the pages of this book on chlorine free paper made with 10% post-consumer waste.

TREES	WATER	SOLID WASTE	GREENHOUSE GASES
8	3,777	229	784
FULLY GROWN	GALLONS	POUNDS	POUNDS

Calculations based on research by Environmental Defense and the Paper Task Force. Manufactured at Friesens Corporation

FSC
Mixed Sources
Cert no. SW-COC-001271
© 1996 FSC

Library and Archives Canada Cataloguing in Publication

Robertson, Heather, 1942-
    Walking into wilderness : the Toronto Carrying Place and Nine Mile Portage / Heather Robertson.

Includes bibliographical references.
ISBN 978-1-896150-59-8

1. Toronto Carrying Place Trail (Ont.)--History. 2. Nine Mile Portage (Ont.)--History. 3. Indian trails--Ontario, South Central--History. 4. Portages--Ontario, South Central--History. 5. Fur trade--Ontario, South Central--History. 6. Wyandot Indians--Ontario, South Central--History. 7. Ontario, South Central--History. I. Title.

FC3061.R62 2010   971.3   C2010-905208-0

Preeceding page: Painted in April 1825 by British naval officer, artist and naturalist George Back, famous as part of John Franklin's two overland expeditions to the Arctic, this unusual landscape is titled Old decayed trees on the Portage between Lake Simcoe and the Nottawasaga River.

Walking into Wilderness

THE TORONTO CARRYING PLACE
AND
NINE MILE PORTAGE

Heather Robertson

Heartland Associates, Inc.
Winnipeg, Canada

Printed in Manitoba, Canada

Acknowledgements

MY THANKS to the generous companions who have made my journey easier by sharing with me their own research, maps, paintings, photographs, expertise, opinions and wilderness skills: the King Township Historical Society, Library and Museum; Keith H.J. Bacon; Ken Carter; Conrad Heidenreich; Bernie Longson; Ann Love; Lisette Mallet; Madeline McDowell; Peter Monahan; Joyce Park; Paul Pepperall and Barry Wallace.

Heather Robertson, August 2010

Opposite: A moody reflection on the Humber River

WALKING INTO WILDERNESS: THE TORONTO CARRYING PLACE AND NINE MILE PORTAGE

Introduction

APRIL 19, 2009: I am walking along a narrow path through small, scrubby trees on the east bank of the Humber River, not far from the marshy bay where the river empties into Lake Ontario. My guide is Lisette Mallet of La Société d'histoire de Toronto, coordinator of Le Sentier Partagé/The Shared Path, a project to create an interpretive park along the riverbank to honour the historic French presence in Ontario. The first European to arrive in Ontario was a young Frenchman, Étienne Brûlé, who came in 1610. Interpreter, explorer, trader, warrior and diplomat, Brûlé lived among the Wendat or Huron, as they were long known, and Algonquin nations on Georgian Bay in Lake Huron for more than twenty years. Among the numerous woodland trails Brûlé would have used on his travels in the Great Lakes area was the Toronto Carrying Place, a forty-six-kilometre portage from the mouth of the Humber River north across the Oak Ridges Moraine to the West Holland River, from there, by canoe and on foot, to Lake Simcoe and Lake Huron.

The muddy path I am following is a vestige of the Carrying Place's southern terminus, a track that led from a riverbank landing place to a high, dry ridge, which now contains the residential street, Riverside Drive. I live closer to the trail's northern end, not far from where it crossed the moraine, its long-vanished path marked here and there by stone cairns and wooden signs beside the rural roads. I was unaware of its significance until I learned only weeks ago that 2010 was the 400th anniversary of Étienne Brûlé's arrival, and that another romantic, tragic hero of my girlhood, René-Robert Cavelier de La Salle, had crossed the "high mountains" of the moraine in 1680 on his way to the Mississippi River. Mysterious, adventurous, rebellious, both were murdered in the wilderness, and how could any child forget that Brûlé had been eaten.

This morning, Lisette and I are tracking the homestead of the City of Toronto's founding family. No, not John Graves Simcoe, the first lieutenant-governor of Upper Canada, or William Lyon Mackenzie, the city's first mayor. Jean-Baptiste Rousseaux and his wife Margaret were comfortably settled here years before Rousseaux piloted Simcoe's schooner into Toronto Harbour in 1793, decades before Mackenzie arrived in Upper Canada from Scotland. A trader, interpreter, guide, and son-in-law of Mohawk chief Joseph Brant, Rousseaux is remembered today by a shiny white Petro-Canada service station on the southern edge of his property; an Ontario Heritage plaque

Signs at a crossroads west of Newmarket and northwest of King City recall Étienne Brûlé and the ancient portage trail he followed over the Oak Ridges Moraine, in the company of a large party of Algonquin and Wendat warriors.

marking the site of his house has been mistakenly placed in a swamp downriver.

As I listen to the traffic roar along the three expressways crossing the river behind me, a gas station seems an appropriate monument to an historic intersection, and the river, broad, marshy, its banks a tangle of trees and brush, has remained amazingly unchanged. In 1991, Ontario surveyor William Daniels was able to locate, on foot, the site of the Rousseaux house and trading post. It had been eloquently described by Percy J. Robinson in his 1933 book, *Toronto During the French Régime*:

In the eighties of the last century, there was a grassy spot at the foot of the hill, neatly terraced, which was a favourite resort for picnic parties; and there were still, if the writer's memory is not at fault, a number of fruit trees, the remains of the orchard and the cherry trees which used to bloom at the old trading-post … Immediately to the north of the dance-hall known as the 'Silver Slipper', there is a sheltered garden sloping down to the river; fruit trees, perhaps the descendants of Rousseau's own orchard, still flourish there; on the margin of the stream is a building much too modern to merit attention, but erected on the very spot where travellers drew up their canoes for centuries before Rousseau came to the Toronto River; there is no other spot on the east bank of the river where a landing could be made; the bank immediately to the north becomes high and precipitous, and the maps indicate that it was at this point that the Toronto Carrying-Place began.

Right: Symbols in Baby Point's upscale neighborhood celebrate the area's long history.

The Silver Slipper burned down in 1958, and the "modern" building, a small dwelling over a boathouse, is gone; the landing place, now part of Étienne Brûlé Park, is obscured by a bridge and a parking lot. What kind of car would Étienne drive today, I wonder. A souped-up, oversize pickup truck? Would he be here on a spring Sunday morning with a crowd of rollerbladers, cyclists and hikers? If we can believe the censorious reports of the seventeenth-century Roman Catholic missionaries, he'd be snuggled up with a sexy babe. He would not be at Mass.

BARRY WALLACE

Ahead, a precipitous promontory looms over the river. Baby Point, an enclave of expensive homes, is named for a Canadian, Jacques Baby. A wealthy landowner and member of Upper Canada's all-powerful colonial clique in the early nineteenth century, Baby was so perfectly bicultural that he anglicized Jacques to James, but pronounced Baby with the soft, French "ah". Baby Point is the site of an earlier Iroquois village, Teiaiagon, built after the Iroquois had stormed north of Lake Ontario to destroy the Wendat/Huron nation in 1649. Tracing the Toronto Carrying Place, I will be journeying through space, time, and a kaleidoscope of cultures.

May 31, 2009: I am standing outside the fenced grass tennis court that occupies the area on Baby Point where the bark longhouses of Teiaiagon are believed to have stood. No one is playing, and no one seems to be at home in the big stone houses that loom out of a planted forest of oaks and maples. The silence, and the sunlight filtered through the leafy canopy, creates the impression of being underwater. Beside me is a tall figure in a floppy sunhat and a loose, pale cotton dress, Madeleine McDowell, a woman I have come to call the Spirit of the River. An artist, dancer, educator, naturalist, historian and indefatigable walker, Madeleine has lived all her sixty-some years on the Toronto Carrying Place, not far from where Humbercrest Boulevard crosses Dundas Street, and she shares her love for the Humber River Valley with anyone who asks.

Teiaiagon is a mystery. The name means, "it crosses the river", and its existence was documented by the French in the 1670s and 1680s, but when exactly the village was built, then abandoned or destroyed, no one seems to know. The

The site of Teiaiagon is now a tennis court.

Mississauga, a northern Algonquin nation, had occupied the area by 1700, and the site of Teiaiagon has never been archaeologically excavated. Only recently, Madeleine tells me, a gas line construction crew accidentally excavated the shallow grave of a woman identified as Seneca, the Iroquois nation that lived across Lake Ontario from Toronto.

"Ontario" and "Toronto" are Iroquois words. Ontario, it is generally agreed, means "big lake" or "big beautiful lake", although early European mapmakers have called it Tadenac, Lac Contenant,

11

Lac St. Louis, Lac des Entouhonoronons, Lac des Iroquois, Cataraqui, Contario and Lac Frontenac. The meaning of "Toronto", I find, is still the subject of confusion and misunderstanding. In 1891, the city of Toronto's first historian, Dr. Henry Scadding, discussed two meanings in common use: "place of meeting", and "trees in the water". Rather than consulting an Iroquois linguist, Scadding derived his own imaginative speculations from the multiple spellings and interpretations of old European maps and dictionaries.

Scadding writes: " 'Place of Meeting' was supposed to refer to certain gatherings of the Indian bands or tribes at this spot periodically for purposes of traffic, or for hunting expeditions, or it may be for hostile excursions. 'Trees in the water', on the other hand, was imagined with considerable plausibility to be a reference to certain trees which aforetime used to appear here and there along the whole length of our island or peninsula, as it then really was, which trees must have been notable landmarks for canoes, or other small craft then coasting about the edges of our lakes."

Percy Robinson came up with a third theory. He discovered an unsigned French map dating from the 1670s that identified Lake Simcoe as "Lac de Taranto", a label confirmed by a 1689 map by Coronelli who added the notation, "Les Piquets", or "stakes".

The French changed the name of Lac de Taranto to Toronto, then to Lac aux Claies: "fish weir lake", a reference to the large weirs made of

sticks Samuel de Champlain had noted in 1615 at the Narrows draining the lake into Lake Couchiching. Trees or poles in the water would be a simple, logical expression for fish weir, a feat of Aboriginal engineering impressive enough to catch Champlain's eye, and to signify not only the lake, but the Carrying Place up the river from Lake Ontario that led to it.

A fish feast at the end of the trip would have encouraged northbound travellers to pack their heavy canoes, baggage, food, furs, weapons and trade goods up the gravel ridge now aptly known as Humbercrest Boulevard, past an intersecting path, Dundas Street,

to campsites on Black Creek and the Eglinton Flats. Madeleine and I follow this route by foot and by car. The portage has been overlain by a network of city streets and railway lines; north of Dundas, it passes through a gated Danier Leather warehouse, and emerges on to a tiny crescent named for hockey star Phil Esposito. A little farther along, the footpath appears again crossing the Jane Woolner

JOEL WALKER

JOEL WALKER

Community Gardens, a series of vegetable plots in the open space under the steel towers of a hydro right-of-way. Aboriginal artifacts have been found here, Madeleine says, indicating that it was once an ancient campsite.

To the north, we follow a path through a wood and past a froggy pond to the south bank of Black Creek in Smythe Park. The park is named for Conn Smythe, founder of the Toronto Maple Leafs hockey team, who owned a gravel pit in this area and lived on Baby Point, but we are visiting the spot where Lieutenant-Governor Simcoe and his party ate lunch on their exploring expedition up the Carrying Place, which left Rousseaux's house on September 25, 1793. It's hard to imagine the picnic, now that the grass is mowed, and Black Creek is channeled into an ugly concrete drain. Was Simcoe in full dress uniform, with braid and lace and cocked hat? What did they eat for lunch? Potted grouse?

I am being unfair. Like most Canadians, I view the British colonial governors as pompous, selfish aristocrats, but as I try to picture Simcoe and his military escort camping here, I have to admit I know almost nothing about him, not even what he looked like. Except for the annual Simcoe Walk which Madeleine leads along this route every September, he has been virtually obliterated from public memory. It must have taken some gumption for Simcoe to strike off into the bush for Lac aux Claies, which he renamed, and Lake Huron, but why, and why did he travel so slowly? After lunch, his expedition camped for the night about a mile to the northwest, now a wild, secluded area by the Humber River behind the Scarlett Woods Golf Course. Here, Madeleine and I end our day's excursion.

June 12, 2009: North Canal, Holland Marsh. I am sitting in an elegant, seventeen-foot Grumman canoe. Its owner, Gordon Elder, paddles bow, a neighbour, Paul Pepperall, stern. Paul, a retired history teacher and amateur archaeologist, has been walking, skiing and studying the northern reaches of the Toronto Carrying Place for years.

Opposite: At Esposito Drive, Madeleine McDowell talks about the river, and the history she loves.

Guided by McDowell, at left, author Heather Robertson, in black at right, and others walk toward the Black Creek site.

Today, he is taking us to visit the campsite where Simcoe's party spent the night of September 28, 1793, in the midst of what Simcoe's wife Elizabeth called "a terrible bog of liquid mud", adding, "The Indians with some difficulty pushed the canoe the Governor was in through it."

The bog was drained years ago to form the flat, black vegetable gardens of the Holland Marsh, but the water in the canal is brown, turgid, thick with swamp plants and slime. The campsite, a high, sloping green meadow, surrounded by a dark forest, is a striking landmark. We swing north up a small river, and ram our canoe through a dense growth of cattails until we reach solid ground at the base of the slope. Climbing up, I notice that the grass has been mowed, and the meadow is dotted with small, gnarly trees – an old apple orchard. The only other signs of human habitation are some raspberry canes, a bench or two, and some possible rotted remnants of a house. The view is breathtaking, a panorama of misty blue hills, cars creeping like ants along pale roads, a bright sprinkling of miniature houses and barns. I can see the very spot where the Carrying Place ended at the lip of the marsh.

"The Governor went to see a very respectable Indian named 'Old Sail' who lives on a branch of Holland's River," Elizabeth Simcoe notes. "He advised him to return by the eastern branch of it to avoid the swamp."

I can see Old Sail's canoemen pushing Simcoe towards this meeting place on the northern branch of the West Holland River, the chief and his councillors solemnly waiting to greet the governor as he disembarked, sweaty, irritable, his white breeches streaked with black muck. Long before, and after, Simcoe's short visit, this meadow was known as an "Indian burial ground". Was Old Sail giving Simcoe wise advice, or telling him to get lost? On his return from Lake Huron in October, Simcoe did take the eastern path. He then widened it into a road and called it Yonge Street.

June 17, 2009: a farm field on the Oak Ridges Moraine. Bent over, eyes fixed on the ground, I am walking slowly in a furrow between two rows of sprouting corn. My six or seven companions are strung out in a line on either side of me. We are volunteers looking for evidence of native campsites in an area where the Toronto Carrying Place crossed the height of land before descending to the bog, or, before that, glacial Lake Algonquin.

I have never done this before. Our leader, Margie Kenedy, an archaeologist with the Toronto Region Conservation Authority, tells us to look out for bright, shiny flakes, particularly the white chert the First Peoples used to make spear points, and stones that appear to have been shaped into tools or burnt as hearth stones. It seems almost incredible to me that small objects lost or discarded thousands of years ago lie so close to the surface that they can be turned up by a farmer's disc or harrow. We are, literally, breaking new ground: this western area of the moraine has never been archaeologically surveyed, although ancient camps and villages have been found only a few kilometres to the east. Margie has chosen this field because it has the characteristics of a good campsite: close to a trail, a commanding view of the surrounding countryside, a fresh breeze to blow away the bugs, and a stream of clear, cold water.

Patiently, we pace the field. I have no luck. Every stone I pick up is, sigh, a stone. Then suddenly the man walking in the furrow beside me stops, bends over and straightens up with a look of surprised delight: in his hand he holds a shiny, pale, triangular stone point, so bright and clean it might have been crafted yesterday. We flock around to see. Wow! It's exquisite, and at least one Stone Age hunter has been here! Soon, other objects are found: a blackened hearthstone, a smoothed rock that might be a scraper or mortar.

In the next few days, I learn that nearly 200 artifacts have been found on this and adjoining cornfields. It will take many months to clean, sort and identify them but everyone is excited: they might be Archaic, even Paleo-Indian, millennia older than the known sites on the Carrying Place between here and Toronto. Talking with Margie and her colleague, Cathy Crinnion, at the TRCA's Restoration Centre in Woodbridge, I realize that the best way to recreate part of the Toronto Carrying Place as it was 500 years ago is to map the known sites of the series of longhouse villages that lined the east bank of the Humber and East

COURTESY OF THE TORONTO AND REGION CONSERVATION AUTHORITY

Humber Rivers from Woodbridge to an old hamlet, Purpleville. After that, the archaeological record is speculation. It will be years before this area of First Peoples settlement will be proven.

September 19, 2009: Fort Willow, Nottawasaga Valley, western terminus of the Nine Mile Portage. Only a few of the travellers heading north on the Toronto Carrying Place lived beside the pathway or on Lake Simcoe; for most, the lake was a way station on a much longer journey. Simcoe was going to Penetanguishene on Lake Huron, a possible harbour for a naval base, La Salle to

The numerous discoveries on the cornfield are marked with red flags.

the mouth of the Mississippi River; Brûlé had come from Québec via the Ottawa River. At first, I assumed that they all paddled the treacherous Severn or Matchedash River between Lake Couchiching and Lake Huron, but then I learned about a popular shortcut, the Nine Mile Portage between Kempenfelt Bay and Willow Creek, a tributary of the Nottawasaga River that flows into Georgian Bay at Wasaga Beach. Originally a First Nations route to the rich plant and wildlife resources of the vast marsh, the Minesing Swamp in the Nottawasaga Valley, the portage was later used by fur traders, voyageurs and couriers anxious to avoid the Severn River's rapids. Mapmaker David Thompson came this way in the 1820s as he surveyed portions of the boundary between Canada and the United States, Sir John Franklin was here on his way to the Arctic in 1825. The portage, however, is best known for the critical role it played in the War of 1812–1814 as the only supply line to the isolated, beleaguered British garrison on Michilimackinac.

This particular Saturday, the annual Nine Mile Portage Festival, Fort Willow is alive with handsome young men in the scarlet uniforms of the Royal Newfoundland Regiment and the dark blue of the Royal Artillery, the two regiments who, along with some sailors, built the original fort in the spring of 1814. The artillery have cannons, the soldiers carry muskets which they load, fire and reload in front of a crowd of gleeful children. The air smells of gunpowder, and smoke from small campfires where men and women in early nineteenth-century dress stir soups in black iron pots in front of small, white canvas tents. In one tent, a gunsmith casts bullets from molten lead; next door, a woman in a billowy cotton dress weaves cloth by hand. Female weavers, cooks and candle makers would not have been here in 1814, but neither would a crowd of tourists in jeans and sunhats.

Most of us have come here by bus from Barrie. There is a hiking trail from the city, but only short portions of the Nine Mile Portage can be walked or driven; the rest of the portage is farmland, houses or swamp. The last mile was a

ANDREW MARSHALL

muddy track down a steep escarpment from Fort Willow to a landing place on Willow Creek. I can walk part of that trail as far as a railway embankment, but the rest is fenced off. I peer down into the dark green swamp ahead and find twilight, even at high noon. From here, the British troops rowed their bateaux, made at Fort Willow, forty miles down the meandering Nottawasaga River to Lake Huron, then more than 300 miles along the lake's North Channel to successfully defend Fort Michilimackinac from an American naval assault. In retaliation, American warships trapped the last British supply schooner, the *Nancy*, in the mouth of the Nottawasaga River. The *Nancy* was blown up, but the British and Canadians, in bateaux, surprised and captured the two American ships remaining on Lake Huron in a nighttime attack every bloodthirsty pirate would envy.

ANDREW MARSHALL

ANDREW MARSHALL

Opposite: The Nine Mile Portage Festival at Fort Willow

Left: Firing muskets out over Kempenfelt Bay, with Barrie, Ontario, in the distance

Above: A Union Jack flying, festival participants embark by canoe onto Lake Simcoe.

The overgrown shore of the Glengarry Landing site is virtually impossible to spot.

October 14, 2009. Edenvale, Nottawasaga River. This is the last leg of my journey. I have visited Wasaga Beach, renowned for its sweeping crescent of yellow sand, motels, parties and hordes of sunbathers. A quiet museum displays the remains of the *Nancy* in a huge glass box. The Nottawasaga River, brown and weedy, flows around it. I have contemplated the Nottawasaga at various points upstream in its leisurely course through farm fields. It seems to be a drab, rural, unromantic river that belies its warlike Ojibwe name, "Rivermouth of the Iroquois". But I grew up at the junction of two other muddy, subversive rivers, the Red and Assiniboine, a more westerly campsite on the same route that led to the Pacific, Arctic and Atlantic Oceans.

From Edenvale, a canoe launch site, I can reach the junction of Willow Creek and the Nottawasaga River. I want to greet the ghosts of Thompson, Franklin and the nameless, unknown multitudes who have travelled to the ends of the earth through this still pristine swamp. Paul Pepperall has brought his own canoe, and Ann Love, an artist and naturalist, will take photographs. They are both strong, experienced canoe trippers. I get to sit in the middle, holding a map.

Good thing too. As we enter the swamp, we are engulfed by a dense, drowned forest, a monochromatic landscape of greens and browns. It has been an unusually wet summer, and rivulets are running into the river from all directions. I have been warned that canoeists get lost in this watery

labyrinth. I can believe it. We know we're on the Nottawasaga by its surprisingly powerful current as it snakes through the mossy bog, but parts of the river are almost blocked by fallen trees. Fighting the current, Ann and Paul expertly skirt around them, keeping a sharp eye out for a much greater danger – deadheads, half-submerged logs that could snag our canoe and tip it. The muddy brown river is full of them, visible only by the ripples they make in the current. One set of ripples turns out to be a muskrat swimming along the shore.

Above: Five turtle species, including snapping turtles, above, are found in Minesing Swamp, through which Willow Creek wanders to meet the Nottawasaga River.

My canoe route map shows the confluence of Willow Creek to be about three kilometres from our launch site, the third of three streams running into the Nottawasaga on our left. We agree that the first we pass is Marl Creek, marked on my map of the Minesing Swamp as Glengarry Landing, a site where bateaux were apparently built in 1814, but the shore is completely overgrown and there seems to be no sign identifying the creek. This is strange. The Nottawasaga Valley Conservation Authority, stewards of the swamp, promotes the valley as a destination for canoeists, campers, fishermen, bird watchers and nature lovers, but where are we?

We press on. The breeze is cold, the silence eerie: the songbirds have gone south. Sunlight shimmering through the trees casts dark shadows. It's easy to imagine Iroquois lurking there, but we are the only travellers on this surly river; there is no dry place to land to stretch our legs and have a bite to eat. "The Swamp is an isolated wilderness," says a note on my map. "Use appropriate caution and let at least one responsible person know where you are going and when you will return." Paul regrets that we didn't bring a change of dry clothes.

At last, we come to a second creek, if it is a creek at all. We pause and study the trickle of water. It has no name on my map, but big, wiggly Willow Creek should be only a short distance ahead, flowing straight towards us where the Nottawasaga bends sharply to the right. Here,

however, the river is so flooded, so choked with deadfall, that it's difficult to see its course ahead. Oh, surveyor Thompson, where are you when we need you? We peer and ponder. One more push, and we'll turn back.

There it is! A strong, fairly deep stream flows in to the left just as we round the bend. I am convinced it's Willow Creek; Ann and Paul are not so certain. We turn up it to investigate. Look! The water is black! Ink black! We stop, and look at each other, amazed. We have never seen water this weird colour, at least not in Ontario, the Prairies, or the Yukon. Spooky. The water looks clear, not polluted. The only smell is rotting vegetation. Nothing I have read, including my maps, has mentioned this phenomenon.

We have made a discovery! Exhilarated, cold and tired, we ride the current downriver to land safely at our launching site.

Filtered sunlight turns Minesing Swamp's riverside woodlands and dark waters into a fantasy of shimmering emerald.

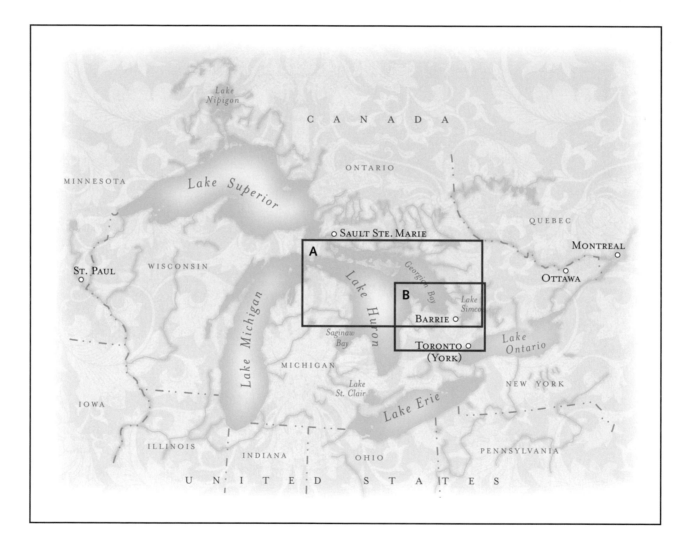

*Opposite page: A map showing
the Great Lakes and contemporary borders*

*Below: Detail of Georgian Bay and Lake Huron
showing the great distances travelled by early traders*

*Right: Detail of the Carrying Place Trail and
Nine Mile Portage, showing the major topographic
landforms travellers encountered*

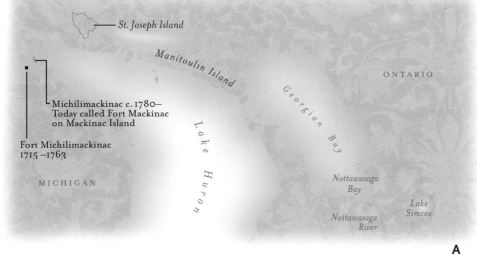

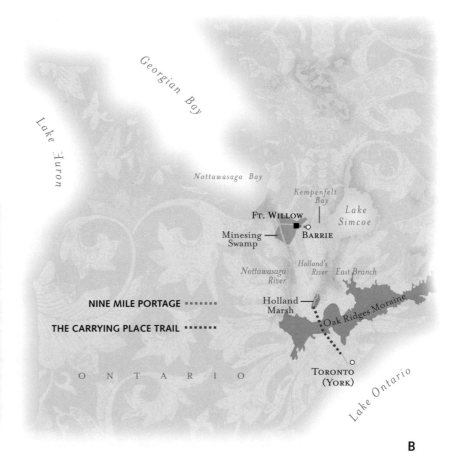

The four-hundred-million-year-old bedrock of Southern Ontario is buried in most places, but visible in the Niagara Escarpment, as here on the shore of Georgian Bay.

Building Southern Ontario

The pathways that lead, by land, river and lake,

from Lake Ontario to Georgian Bay on Lake Huron,

follow a broad trough gouged in ancient bedrock

by runoff water before a series of glaciations,

beginning about two million years ago,

filled it with sand, clay and muck

ground from the rocks themselves.

Archean-Paleoproterozoic cartonic nuclei

Grenvillian orogenic belts

Between 750 and 725 million years ago, Rodinia began to break up, forming Laurentia, or ancestral North America, (seen here astride the equator at the centre of the map) as well as East and West Gondwana.

THE LAURENTIAN RIVER or Channel, as it is called, once drained the upper Great Lakes area from Georgian Bay into the Lake Ontario basin, the St. Lawrence River and the Atlantic Ocean, and though this watershed is much changed on the surface, it still defines southern Ontario.

The region's buried bedrock of limestone and shale – invisible except for outcrops such as the Niagara Escarpment – is between 400 and 470 million years old, but young compared to the Precambrian Archaen rock to the north. As Earth's crust was hardening about 2.5 billion years ago, most of Canada was part of a continent we know as Arctica, an agglomeration of granite masses, including Siberia and Greenland, that had crashed together as they drifted on a sea of dark, volcanic basalt that had spewed from Earth's molten core. Over the next billion years, Arctica grew to include most of North America, Europe and Antarctica. Geologists have renamed this huge continent Nena, and it lay between two other primeval continents on Earth's shifting surface. To the west lay Ur (comprised of India, Australia and part of South Africa), while Atlantica (South America and West Africa) lay to the southeast. When Atlantica violently collided with Nena about 1.3 billion years ago to form Rodinia – one of at least four "supercontinents" in Earth's long history – the impact on Nena's southeast coast threw up mountain ranges of twisted, contorted rocks, chemically transformed by the intense heat and pressure of tectonic upheavals that lasted a million years.

This rugged frontier, known as the Grenville province, was southern Ontario's original landscape, but it didn't last long. By 800 million years ago, the Grenville mountains had eroded away into a flat, scoured plain, still visible in Muskoka and on the east shore of Georgian Bay; within another 300 million years, Rodinia had broken up, and southern Ontario was flooded by the warm, shallow waters of the Iapetus Ocean.

As the ocean floor sagged and sank, this shallow basin collected layers of sediment, providing a sheltered environment for teeming aquatic life. Tall forests of sea lilies were home to a host of exotic creatures: trilobites, molluscs, brachiopods, gastropods, worms and jellyfish. Corals built reefs and, over a period of 100 million years, the ocean bed hardened into fossilized limestone.

Then, in another catastrophic collision, what is now Europe slammed onto the east coast of North America. The impact blocked the Iapetus Ocean, and clouds of hot, black ash that spewed from a new range of volcanoes, the Taconic Mountains, fell into the pristine water. This subtropical environment was lashed by hurricanes, eroding the mountains and covering the Simcoe Group limestones with a thick layer of softer, blue-gray shales of the Georgian Bay and Queenston Formations. As Earth's convulsions continued over millions of years, continents collided and fused to form another supercontinent, Pangaea. About 150 million years ago, Pangaea began to break apart, gradually forming the oceans and continents we know today. The limestones and shales of southern Ontario were heaved up out of the water and exposed to millions of years of erosion.

Glaciers have been part of Earth's history for almost two billion years as continents drifted over, or close to, the North and South Poles. The ice sheets that most recently shaped Canadian topography formed in the Arctic about 10 million years ago. "This process culminated in the development of large ice sheets on a continental scale in North America and Europe," University of Toronto geologist Nick Eyles writes in *Ontario Rocks.*

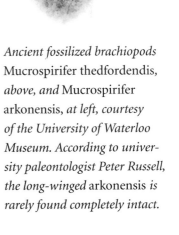

Ancient fossilized brachiopods Mucrospirifer thedfordendis, *above, and* Mucrospirifer arkonensis, *at left, courtesy of the University of Waterloo Museum. According to university paleontologist Peter Russell, the long-winged* arkonensis *is rarely found completely intact.*

THE KEY EVENT that triggered glaciation was the collision of India with Eurasia, which forced up the Himalayan Mountains. This changed global circulation patterns in the atmosphere and the way in which heat moved from the equator to the poles. Simultaneously, large amounts of sediment were washed off the rapidly eroding mountains. The weathering of this sediment consumed carbon dioxide that would otherwise have warmed Earth's atmosphere and contributed to slow cooling. The joining of North and South America about 3.5 million years ago by the formation of the Isthmus of Panama closed what had previously been a gateway between the two continents. This changed circulation in the North Atlantic Ocean, increasing the delivery of warm water and moisture to the northern latitudes. Moisture is the key ingredient in the formation of ice sheets.

Opposite: In places, Ontario still looks much as it might have more than 100,000 years ago.

Built by heavy snowfalls and sub-zero temperatures lasting thousands of years, glaciers would grow, depressing Earth's crust under their great weight and grinding the underlying rock, soil and vegetation into a lumpy, concrete-like till. Then, like the swing of a pendulum, the climate would warm and the melting ice would run off as rivers and pool into lakes.

The most extensive and varied record of glacial activity in southern Ontario was discovered in 1962 in a fifteen-metre railway cut west of the Humber River and south of the town of Woodbridge. CNR construction crews had sliced through a layer cake of glacial till deposited during two glaciations beginning 135,000 years ago. By determining the type of till or silt, geologists are able to track the path of glaciers that vanished long ago.

In the Woodbridge deposit, the earlier of the two most recent ice sheets, the Illinoian, had first deposited dark, heavy mud known as York Till, and this, in turn, was covered by thinner soil of sandy clay of Sangamon age, about 125,000 years old, containing fossils: the earliest evidence of life in the Humber River valley. In 2001, an inter-disciplinary team of scientists led by geologist Paul Karrow of the University of Waterloo, completed a thirty-five-year analysis of the Woodbridge formation. In the Sangamon soil, formed between 125,000 to 80,000 years old, they found pine, maple and birch tree pollen, molluscs, minute crustaceans called ostracodes, insects, the tooth of a pike, shrews, voles, mice and four fossilized garter snakes, only the second reptile find of this age in Ontario. The landscape, they concluded, had been wooded, with temporary ponds, on a floodplain with a nearby stream. The climate of the Sangamon interglacial was mild, probably a little warmer than today. Later, soils from this period were overlain by layers of tills containing ice wedges, evidence of long and repeated interludes of ground frost and glaciation prior to North America's most recent glacial period, the Late Wisconsinan.

THE OAK RIDGES MORAINE

THE ONSET of the late Wisconsin glaciation about 26,000 years ago created a colder climate in southern Ontario (and elsewhere in Canada), which initially encouraged an environment of wet, boreal forest of spruce and balsam fir, heaths, herbs and mosses. Over the next six millennia, the forest became dry, sparse tundra bordering deep, frigid lakes that pooled at the edge of the advancing ice sheet. By 20,000 BP, North America's most recent continental glacier, the Laurentide, had buried all of southern Ontario under between 500 and 1000 metres of ice. This enormous sheet of ice covered what are now the Great Lakes for 7,000 years and it was the Laurentide's reluctant, hesitant retreat, beginning about 13,000 BP, which created the idiosyncratic, but temperate and hospitable inter-lake landscape that has become, within the last century, one of the most prosperous and densely populated areas in North America.

As the Laurentide ice sheet melted, it split into lobes. Rivers of meltwater deposited their heavy loads of till into the glacial crevasses, forming sand ridges, deltas and moraines. Most significant is the Oak Ridges Moraine. Stretching 160 kilometres from the Niagara Escarpment in the west to the Trent River in the east, it separates the watershed of Lake Ontario from that of Lake Huron. On its southern slope, innumerable springs, streams, kettle lakes and marshes form the headwaters of the Humber, Don and Rouge Rivers; to the north, the Holland River flows into Lake Simcoe, and from there the Severn River flows to Georgian Bay on Lake Huron. Up to twenty kilometres wide and 300 metres high, the hilly, hummocky moraine formed a natural boundary between two glacial lakes, Lake Iroquois to the south, Lake Algonquin to the north.

The ghost of Lake Iroquois is visible in Toronto's Scarborough Bluffs and Davenport Road, which follows the lake's ancient beach, ends in an enormous bar of sand and gravel northeast of where Dundas Street West meets the Humber River. (As indicated on page 172, this, ultimately, became Conn Smythe's gravel pit.) To the north, the dramatic sand dunes and beaches of Nottawasaga Bay were created by northwesterly winds and waves as Lake Algonquin

Lake Simcoe

Oak Ridges Moraine

Lake Ontario

TORONTO

BARBARA ENDRES

shrank into Lake Huron and Lake Simcoe. Between the two lakes, ridges and hills – former beaches and islands – are surrounded by the sand and clay flats of the old lake bottom; in the middle is Minesing Swamp, once a small, landlocked lake.

Southwestern Ontario emerged as an island surrounded by glacial lakes that fluctuated in size and depth as the Laurentide ice sheet retreated to the north; when the outlet to the St. Lawrence River valley became exposed some 12,000 years ago, Lake Iroquois drained away to a puddle much smaller than Lake Ontario is today. As the bedrock began to rebound from the weight of the ice, lake water cut channels and settled into the deepest basins and rifts in the continent's now scarred and weathered skin, creating the Great Lakes as they are today.

The climate rapidly warmed. Arctic and boreal plants returned to this reborn landscape, followed by mastodons and woolly mammoths, winterized

descendants of Proboscideans, among Earth's dominant large herbivorous or plant eating creatures for more than twenty million years and ancestors to today's elephants. Along with giant beaver, giant short-faced bears, stag moose and horses, along with other large mammals, they had survived the Pleistocene epoch's climatic vagaries for nearly two million years, only to disappear very soon after the Wisconsin glaciation. Scientists have long wondered why, for these megafauna had survived dramatic climate change many times before. Now, however, global warming came in combination with predators that were apparently harmless, but armed with deadly weapons and devious ideas: humans.

The map, opposite, illustrates the glacial cravass that allowed the formation of the Oak Ridges Moraine, above left.

Southern Ontario was long a haven for woolly mammoths, above, and mastodons.

Free-flowing water, climax forests, abundant wildlife and rich glacial soil made life
in ancient Ontario not only possible but, ultimately, bountiful.

Early People

Early people trekked north of Lake Erie

and Lake Ontario between 10,500 and 12,000

years ago, possibly following the banks of streams

flowing from fertile southern regions

that had escaped the glacier's grasp.

Fine-grained and rich in silica, white chert, prized for its lustrous density and ability to hold a sharp edge, was widely traded. The beaked scraper, at right, was used on wood or animal hides, while the small graver, a portion of which is shown below, was likely used to drill holes in hides. Found by archaeologist Peter Storck, both date to between 12,000 and 10,000 years ago.

WHO WERE THEY, and why did they come to this intimidating, unknown frontier? Were they explorers, adventurers, outcasts, refugees? Or were they hunters pursuing herds of migrating caribou? Apart from their distinctive fluted spear points, chipped from hard flint or chert, and other stone tools they left at their campsites, we know almost nothing about the first inhabitants. Their spear points are known as Clovis, Folsom, Barnes and Gainey, after locations in the United States where they were first found, often at sites where giant bison and mammoths, now long extinct, had been slaughtered. Artists have created romantic images of small, muscular, brown men clad in animal skins spearing monstrous, rampaging beasts with their flimsy homemade weapons, but some archaeologists now speculate that early people may have scavenged dead or dying animals, or trapped them in bogs and ravines. Mammoth and mastodon bones have been unearthed at numerous locations in southern Ontario, but no spear points have been found with the bones. Whether they succumbed to environmental stress or human hunger, mammoths, mastodons and giant beaver disappeared as a food supply very soon after the people arrived.

Caribou survive to this day in northern Ontario's boreal forests and tundra regions, and caribou may have made the post-glacial trails that humans followed north. For thousands of years, caribou have provided Canada's northern peoples with nourishing meat, fat and bone marrow, hides to make tents, warm clothing and water-proof boots, sinew for sewing and fastening, bone for tools and weapons. The caribou's annual migrations from the shelter of spruce forests to the tundra and back are predictable, although their numbers vary, their routes change and they run so fast that human hunters have to dream of the most likely places to intercept them.

A vision of ghostly caribou inspired Peter Storck, a young archaeologist with the Royal Ontario Museum, to begin a systematic search for early human sites in the area between Nottawasaga Bay and Lake Simcoe in the summer of 1974. A few years before, a farmer, Edward Banting, had found two fluted spear points on a hill at the back of his property near the town of Alliston. Realizing that the hill had been an island in glacial Lake Algonquin, Storck speculated that the hunters had chosen this vantage point for a specific reason. "I planned to concentrate my search for campsites on higher terrain overlooking possible fording places where caribou might have crossed narrow bodies of water," he writes in *Journey to the Ice Age*, "and at the southern ends of the major arms of the lake where caribou might have passed if they had been deflected in their movements by broad expanses of water."

The following summer, armed with geological maps, Storck and his crew began to survey an eighty-kilometre stretch of Lake Algonquin's ancient shoreline from Glencairn, west of Barrie on Lake Simcoe, to Thornbury on Nottawasaga Bay.

Majestic and able to live in boreal forest environments most other ungulates find impossible, woodland caribou once thrived from Ontario's northern taiga south into the northeastern United States.

BARBARA ENDRES

JERRY KAUTZ

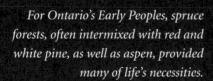

For Ontario's Early Peoples, spruce forests, often intermixed with red and white pine, as well as aspen, provided many of life's necessities.

On a farm owned by the Fisher family south of the town of Stayner, they found one of the most productive early sites in North America: more than 150 scrapers, spokeshaves, engravers, hammerstones and fluted points, with flakes and debris indicating that they had been manufactured at the site. More significantly, they had been painstakingly chipped from an unusual white chert, identical to tools and weapons archaeologists were finding at Parkhill, a site 175 kilometres to the southwest. These people were clearly related, possibly the same band, but where had they mined the stone?

In 1979, invertebrate paleontologist Peter von Bitter found the source of the chert in a small outcrop of the Fossil Hill Formation on the shore of Nottawasaga Bay. Had these early people come north in pursuit, not of caribou, but of a superior Stone Age technology? It appeared that they camped by Lake Algonquin during the summer, when the area was free of snow, returning south, with their bags of new implements, for the winter.

WHAT WERE the women doing? No one knows. As the men were flintknapping on the hill, keeping an eye out for deer and grizzly bears, their wives, mothers and children may have been fishing, gathering eggs from goose nests or picking buffaloberries among the poplars and birches on the windswept beach. They probably preferred to camp in valleys near ponds and streams, all evidence of their presence long buried in silt and decaying vegetation, or drowned by rising water.

In sheltered spruce forests, they would have found dry branches for firewood and small game animals, such as hares, foxes and squirrels, to skin and cook; women might have woven baskets from red osier dogwood, and harvested freshwater clams, crayfish and turtles. Though insects, especially the blackflies, were irritating, and the food supply barely sufficient to support a transient population of a few hundred people, their feet, bare or moccasined, made Ontario's first human paths.

Evidence of ancient campsites near kettle lakes on top of the Oak Ridges Moraine indicate that the Early Peoples walked north across the dry bottom of what is now Lake Ontario, then crossed the moraine up the Humber and Rouge rivers to the shores of shrinking Lake Algonquin's southern lagoons. At that time, Lake Ontario, a remnant of glacial Lake Iroquois, was about 100 metres lower than it is today, exposing 10,000 square kilometres of rock and soil. The water had drained in a rush into the St. Lawrence Valley, but as the weight of the ice lifted, and the rocks to the northeast rebounded, Lake Ontario began to flood again.

"The late Ice Age was a period of rapid, even catastrophic environmental change," writes Storck. "Some of this occurred not over millennia or even centuries but perhaps just over decades, a few years, even hours: local extinctions, bursting ice dams and sudden floods, and regional temperature and vegetation reversals. The Ice Age world was a dangerous place."

Clay pots, decorated around the neck with patterns made with cord, sticks or shells, appeared in Southern Ontario about 2,800 years ago. Archaeologists believe the three shown here were influenced by different cultures: above, the Wendat; at right, the Seneca, and below, the Petun. All, however, are from the Seed-Barker Site (see page 44).

PHOTOS: BARRY WALLACE

The hot southern winds that melted the glaciers soon transformed the barren grounds into an upland forest of pines and oaks, with tamarack, white cedar and black spruce on the lowlands, and by 8,000 years ago, the climate of southern Ontario was much as it is today – hot, humid summers and cold winters with heavy, wet snow south of Lake Huron. Verdant forests of maple, ash, elm, beech, hemlock, hickory, basswood and walnut provided the Early and Middle Archaic people, as we call them, with hardwoods, nuts, fruits and woodland game – deer, bear, elk, beaver, muskrat – to spear or trap; they fished with nets and bone hooks.

Was life now too comfortable? They created stone axes and other woodworking implements, notched rather than fluted their projectile points and experimented with a variety of polished rocks, but they remained a Stone Age people for millennia until, about 5,500 years ago, they acquired copper from the western shore of Lake Superior. Whether they traded for copper knives, scrapers and beads, or manufactured them, copper indicated a revolution in both technology and travel; Great Lakes people had the ability to transport trade goods hundreds of kilometres, either by water, in dugout canoes, or across the ice by snowshoe, toboggan and dog team. The presence in Late Archaic burial sites of both western copper and ornamental shells from the Atlantic Ocean indicates a communication network that may have extended west to the wild rice lakes of the Mississippi River watershed.

Crudely made clay pots, useful for storing wild rice, dried berries and fish oil, appeared in Southern Ontario about 2,800 years ago. Their rough decorations, pressed into the soft clay with cords, sticks or shells, reflected a variety of regional cultures which, while still on the move, stored some of their food in central locations, probably cemetery campsites. These communal graves, with their ceremonial red ochre pigment and buried treasures of bead necklaces, silver and copper implements and musical panpipes, as well as stone carvings of birds and animals are among the few permanent legacies of the vanished Woodland peoples. Governed by the ritual cycles of seasons, they understood past and future time.

Yet they developed two different cultures with mutually unintelligible languages: Algonquian and Iroquoian. How these two peoples came to share a relatively small area, the Algonquian on the southwest shores of Lake Huron, the Iroquoian north of Lake Erie and Lake Ontario, has provoked decades of controversy and speculation. Were the Iroquoian invaders from the east and south, who pushed the indigenous people aside, or did they evolve their own culture by importing ideas and technology most adaptable to the fertile lands where they lived?

Noting that the cultivation of maize was introduced into Ontario about 1,500 years ago, centuries prior to the emergence of a complex, sophisticated Iroquoian longhouse society, Toronto archaeologist Ron Williamson believes that it is likely that "a small number of Iroquoian speakers introduced both maize and the language to resident Algonquian-speaking Great Lakes populations after which both the language and the subsistence technology gained wide-spread acceptance." Clustered in small, mobile camps near the mouths of the creeks and rivers on Lake Ontario's north shore, the newcomers lived much like their Algonquian neighbours: fishing, hunting, gathering fruits and nuts, raising a few vegetables and a little maize to store over the winter.

The region's light, well-drained soils were well suited to the cultivation of corn, beans, squash, sunflowers and tobacco, crops that had been grown for millennia in Central America; after centuries of experimentation, the Ontario Iroquoian settled down to become farmers. The Algonquian, however, remained a mobile, maritime people: hunters, fishers, travellers and traders, although the Nottawasaga River watershed appears to have been a common, friendly frontier.

Maize, squash (above, with pumpkin seeds at left) and beans — were the "three sisters" of early agriculture. They were often planted together; the cornstalk provided support for the climbing beans, and shade for the squash. The squash vines covered the ground, limiting weeds, and the beans fixed nitrogen for all three crops.

All three were grown in the Americas for thousands of years, but the original varieties have been all but lost. To preserve these rare plants, a number of North America's historic sites, including Ontario's Sainte-Marie among the Hurons and Nebraska's Museum of the Fur Trade, cultivate and preserve heritage varieties.

COURTESY OF THE MUSEUM OF THE FUR TRADE, CHADRON, NEBRASKA

LONGHOUSE VILLAGES

EARLY IN THE FOURTEENTH CENTURY AD, a social revolution transformed the Iroquoian culture and the landscape of Lake Ontario's north shore. Over the next 300 years, families living in scattered clusters of small, rivermouth camps merged to create large, longhouse villages on the higher ground of the moraine's south slope. The boldest migrants seem to have leapfrogged the moraine entirely to settle on the fertile highlands between Lake Simcoe and Georgian Bay; many relocated along the east bank of the Humber River near the present communities of Woodbridge and Kleinburg. The arrival in the Gulf of St. Lawrence of European sailors and fishing fleets in the early sixteenth century may have contributed to this upheaval; between Jacques Cartier's last visit in 1535 and Samuel de Champlain's first in 1603, the Iroquoian population of the lower St. Lawrence River vanished. Linguistic and ceramic evidence suggests that some of them moved into Ontario, and they may have brought new tools and ideas with them.

Immigration and a healthy local diet contributed to a population explosion that must have depleted the seasonal resources; feuds among bands or families over dwindling food supplies might have precipitated their coalescence into hostile strongholds. The virgin northern woods offered plentiful timber and bark for construction, black bear, beaver and herds of white-tailed deer, and, once cleared, broad, rolling fields and floodplains for corn and vegetables. These new villages were planned, defended, and firmly dug into the ground.

A cluster of cigar-shaped bark longhouses, situated most frequently on a bluff or plateau beside the river or a tributary such as Black Creek, was enclosed by a double palisade of vertical poles, spaced about twenty centimetres apart and planted in a trench with a single entrance gate. One longhouse, perhaps for visitors, was often placed outside the palisade. Inside, the houses varied in length from ten to twenty-eight metres, with an average width of 7.5 metres. They were crowded; a row of cooking fires ran down the middle, with two families sharing each hearth. Holes in the concave roof let out the smoke, but the longhouses had no windows, and people slept among their belongings by the walls. One end of the longhouse was a communal storeroom; the space between the palisades served as a garbage dump.

In spite of the stifling smoke, the longhouses must have been warm in the depths of winter, when temperatures could reach -40° C, and the residents were probably relatives, perhaps a family of sisters, their parents, husbands and children.

Tanned furs and a large hearth meant winter wamth, while cornmeal or beans stored in large ceramic pots helped feed longhouse residents when snow lay deep on the ground.

A supply of dried corn, pounded into coarse flour and boiled into gruel, would feed them, with little effort, in lean seasons when game and fish were scarce. Women and children spent most of the year in the fields, planting, hoeing and harvesting the crops; men may have done the fishing, although drying or smoking the fish was likely women's work. The addition of vegetables, sunflower oil and cornstarch to a high protein meat diet must have contributed to the founding of new villages and the expansion of the old; new fields had to be cleared and villages moved every ten to fifty years as the unfertilized soil became depleted; without cattle, these farmers had no manure.

Society became organized into matriarchal clans, with male chiefs, and defined identities; in the Blue Mountains of Collingwood, the Etionnon-tateronnon – "People where there is a hill or a mountain" – specialized in trading tobacco, a luxury crop much in demand. The French named them "Petun". Numerous and aggressive, the Wendat, later known as "Huron" by the French, were warlike, while the Hatiwendaronk – "people who have distinct words, voice" – remained in the Niagara Peninsula where, as the "Neutral", they tried to keep the peace between the Wendat and their Seneca enemies on the Genesee River south of Lake Ontario.

How could agricultural, Iroquoian, longhouse peoples, who seemed to have everything in common, fight to the death? Had some Wendat ancestors been driven north by a family feud, which was then fuelled for centuries by a cycle of revenge? Neither possessed mines of gold and silver or

The large multi-family long-houses were shingled on the exterior with long slabs of bark from southern Ontario's once-mighty forests.

COURTESY OF THE SIMCOE COUNTY MUSEUM

anything else of great value the other could not produce or acquire by trade, and both had to protect their flanks against powerful Algonquian tribes. Warfare may simply have been part of their social and political networks, a ritualized way of giving restless, energetic young men something thrilling to do in the summer, away from home.

War was a lethal game of hide-and-seek. Sneaking into the enemy's territory, warriors lurked in the woods and waited for a chance to abduct women from the cornfields, or massacre an unwary family out fishing. Victims were clubbed and scalped on the spot, or taken captive; some were adopted into the enemy band, perhaps to replace a dead relative, the rest were ceremonially tortured to death. If the invaders themselves were discovered and captured, they suffered the same fate. Evidence of cowardice or weakness in the enemy might precipitate a mass attack on the village: palisades could be scaled or set afire, the bark longhouses torched by flaming arrows. Or the inhabitants might burn their village themselves and flee to neighbouring communities.

These societies of intermarried, matrilineal clans were organized into chiefs, councils, medicine societies, including semi-subterranean sweat lodges, feasts and seasonal rituals. Like all villages, they had distinct personalities and power structures, but, when relocating, they shared a common practice of disinterring their dead and reburying the cleaned bones together in a pit, or ossuary. The Kleinburg Ossuary, excavated in 1970, yielded the remains of 561 individuals, buried with iron axes, kettles and glass beads obtained by trade with Europeans.

Nearby, on a site he calls Damiani, archaeologist Ron Williamson and his team recently found fragments of discarded human bones, an indication of warfare. There is no evidence that these bones had been deliberately shaped or modified, but cut, polished and perforated human bones, especially skulls, have been found in other locations of the same era, including the Parsons site near York University. At least some of these fifteenth- and sixteenth-century people apparently followed the common Iroquoian practice of decapitating their slain enemies and transforming their skulls into ceremonial rattles or personal talismans. To the south on the East Humber, another site, Seed-Barker, has yielded pipe bowls carved into stylized animal and human heads, although art of this era might well reflect European influence.

As they organized and settled, these agriculturalists developed into three allied nations. By the seventeenth century, two of them had vacated the north shore of Lake Ontario to occupy the area between Georgian Bay, Lake Simcoe and the swamps of the Nottawasaga River. Despite the efforts of the Neutral to deter war, devastating Seneca raids in the sixteenth century may have persuaded the Wendat to abandon their communities on the Oak Ridge Moraine's southern rivers and retreat north of the Nottawasaga watershed to a distant, more defendable peninsula between Lake Simcoe and Georgian Bay. It was here, on the southern shore of Georgian Bay, that the first European, Étienne Brûlé, came to live with them in the summer of 1610.

THE SEED-BARKER SITE

Looking northeast toward the raised plateau, the Seed-Barker Site, opposite, is quiet today. Between 1450 and 1600, however, it was home to thousands.

Below, a plan of the Seed-Barker Site.

Fence Line

Cultivated lands

APPROX. 30 RODS

ash beds

APPROX. 20 RODS

Cultivated lands

Fence Line

Fence Line

No remains were found east of this line

Cultivated lands

Legend:
- ▨ Excavated house wall
- — Extrapolated house wall
- ⋯ Presumed house wall

THE PALISADED VILLAGES that crowned the bluffs northeast of the junction of the East and West Humber Rivers between 1450 and 1600 AD can be imagined today because their residents broke a lot of crockery, and left their tools lying around. In the nineteenth century, European immigrants tilling these fields often turned up strange-looking, handworked stones, bits of terracotta pottery and tobacco pipes with broken stems, their bowls carved into human and animal effigies. If the farmers didn't toss these weird objects away, they displayed them in a curio cabinet, or on the mantelpiece, and passed them down to their heirs.

Early in the 1880s, Joseph Smelser, a farmer and amateur archaeologist in the village of Laskay on the Oak Ridges Moraine, joined forces with another enthusiast, Rowland Orr, to make a systematic investigation of the area north of Toronto. "For many years," Orr writes, "we spent much time seeking out the ash beds, and opening the ossuaries throughout the townships of Vaughan, York, Markham and King, as well as making incursions into the County of Simcoe. Many of the surface finds were secured by going over the newly sown wheat fields in the fall, after a nice rain. Axes and adzes were frequently found on the fences, placed there by the farmers. Most of the specimens found were from village sites that had been absolutely uncontaminated by European contact."

One of the most dramatic sites Orr and Smelser explored was a raised, sloped plateau, surrounded by rolling hills, on a bend in the East Humber north of the little milltown of Woodbridge in Vaughan township. The Barker site, named after its owner, possessed the essential attributes for an early Wendat/Huron village – good defence, fresh water and fertile soil – and when Orr excavated an ancient ash pit, he found several rare, beautifully finished bone awls.

Orr and Smelser donated all of the artifacts they collected, along with Orr's notes, to the province's new Archaeological Museum in Toronto. There they sat, ignored, for nearly fifty years. When J. Norman Emerson, a professor of anthropology at the University of Toronto, excavated the

For decades, students helped to excavate the Seed-Barker Site, learning that archaeology requires patience and precision. The rewards, opposite, include the discovery of beautifully made pipes and pottery unseen for centuries. Inset: A hanging screen is used to comb the soil for artifacts.

site with a team of students in 1951, it was being devastated by a gravel pit operation that had already revealed and destroyed a number of graves. Yet digging into the remaining middens, Emerson recovered pottery so varied and inventive in its decorations, the site, renamed Seed-Barker for both its owners, was soon recognized as one of the most significant Iroquoian villages in Ontario. Fortunately, Emerson's museum collection of pottery was studied and appreciated by Canada's first, young professional archaeologists, but vandalism and gravel extraction continued at the site until 1975, when the Metro Toronto Regional Conservation Authority incorporated Seed-Barker into the Boyd Conservation Area.

From 1983 until 2005, the ghostly village came back to life as a summer archaeological field school for university and secondary school students. Supervised and instructed by experts, the students excavated the site by hand, trowelling, screening, mapping and identifying artifacts, hearths, post-holes and other traces of human habitation. Laborious hours in the blazing sun were balanced by lectures on cultural history, group discussions, workshops on stone tool manufacture and excursions into the adjacent marsh to identify native plants. One goal of the three-week program was to encourage the students to project themselves back into the Aboriginal culture that created the curious things they were unearthing.

Over the twenty-three year period, more than 1,000 students located vestiges of eight palisade walls, seven complete longhouses, elements of thirteen more structures, and more than one

million artifacts, the vast majority of them fragments of stone, bone and ceramics. Each of four of the houses has five hearths, suggesting ten families or about fifty inhabitants; since most of the site has been destroyed, the population has been estimated as high as 3,000.

Yet this crowded village was only one of at least five built within a few hundred metres of each other between 1450 and 1600 AD. Our knowledge of the others so far is sketchy; one, Skandatut, has been surveyed but not excavated, and a second, Boyd, had been disturbed when located in 1970. Did these villages co-exist for periods of time, or succeed each other? Was Seed-Barker typical, or unique? Several of the bark longhouses were built so close together that their walls almost touched, a grave fire hazard that may have been caused by a

sudden influx of immigrants. The hypothesis that this was a cosmopolitan, innovative community of Wendat/Huron, Petun, Neutral (or, in the Wendat language, Hatiwendaronk – 'they have distant words or voices') and Seneca peoples is supported by the extraordinary variety of pottery styles, and that local potters strengthened their traditional designs to compensate for the poor clay of the Humber Valley.

The sixteenth century was a time of tribal warfare and dramatic population dislocation throughout eastern North America. Were the people who lived on this beautiful plateau from about AD 1520 to 1570 contented artisans, or persecuted refugees? By 1600 they were gone. Who knows where?

The bowls of two pipes, above from left, a pottery handle and an incised and decorated pot are among more than a million artifacts found at the Seed-Barker Site.

Georgian Bay sparkles in the autumn sunshine, displaying one of its many moods.

The French

Étienne Brûlé is the shadowy hero

of a murder mystery unsolved after 377 years.

Adventurer, interpreter, fur trader, Brûlé is known

only through the oblique and usually scathing

words of others; if he kept journals or made maps,

they have been lost or destroyed.

Champlain's sketch of his unsuccessful assault on Carantouan, an Iroquoian village, in 1615. Like many villages in Eastern North America, as well as Mexico and Central America, it was well defended by a double-walled stockade and placed in close proximity to a dependable source of water.

EVEN THE date and place of his birth are uncertain: the *Dictionary of Canadian Biography* guesses 1592, at a village near Paris, Champigny-sur-Marne. Others believe it may have been as late as 1595, and Brûlé's patron and commander, Samuel de Champlain, consistently refers to Brûlé as one of the "boys", or "young boys", he brought to New France to learn the native languages. Since it was common for boys as young as eleven or twelve to be apprenticed to a trade, or sent to sea as cabin boys, Brûlé may have been only thirteen or fourteen when he chose to live among the people of North America, those known by Champlain and others as "the men of the wilderness", *les sauvages.*

He had been lucky to survive two years with Champlain in New France. Sixteen of the twenty-four men who had felled the trees and sawn the boards to build their spartan little habitation at Québec had died the first winter, apparently of scurvy. Brûlé may have supplemented his deadly diet of dried peas and salt pork with native foods, but the Algonquin Montagnais among whom they lived were themselves reduced to eating carrion.

In the spring of 1609, relieved by a shipload of men and supplies sent by his trading partner, Gravé du Pont, Champlain and two Frenchmen joined a war party of Algonquin and "Huron", as the French named the Wendat people, on a bold expedition up the Richelieu River into the very homeland of the Iroquois, historic enemies of the Montagnais. Champlain and his men carried secret weapons – long-barreled guns. Taking the Iroquois by surprise, Champlain killed two chiefs with the first shot from his arquebus, and their warriors fled in terror at the noise. The next summer, Étienne Brûlé was present during the defeat and rout of a second Iroquois encampment near the mouth of the Richelieu River. Watching the fate of the Iroquois, he would have had no illusions about the consequences of antagonizing his triumphant Wendat and Algonquin hosts. Champlain writes:

Seizing their prisoners they took them to the water's edge and tied them upright to a stake. Then each came along with a birch-bark torch, burning them now in one part, now in another; and the poor wretches, feeling the fire, would utter such loud cries, that it was awful to hear, and indeed the cruelties which these barbarians practice upon one another are terrible. Having made them suffer in this way for some time, especially by burning them with this bark, they took water and threw it over their bodies to make them suffer still more. Then they would again apply the fire in such a way that the skin would fall from their bodies, and the captors would continue with loud shouts and whoops, dancing about, until these poor wretches fell dead on the spot.

As soon as one would fall to the ground, they would pound the body violently with clubs; then they would cut off arms, legs and other parts of the body, and amongst them no one was esteemed worthy who did not cut off a piece of flesh and give it to the

dogs. Such is the courtesy which prisoners receive. Nevertheless, they endure all the tortures inflicted on them with such constancy that those who see them are struck with astonishment.

The next day, an Algonquin chief, Iroquet, and a Wendat, Ochataguin, arrived from the west with eighty men, sorry to be too late to participate in the attack, but full of admiration for their good friends, the Christians. They had earlier urged Champlain to visit their country to see for himself a lake as big as the sea, with copper mines and other treasures, and, as proof, had given him a bar of pure copper, melted and smoothed with stones. Could this lake be the Western Sea, the fabulous passage to the Orient the English were eagerly seeking in the frozen Arctic? As Champlain writes:

I had with me, a youth who had already spent two winters at Québec who wished to go with the Algonquins to learn their language. Pont-Gravé and I decided that if he were so disposed, it would be better to send him there than elsewhere, to learn what their country was like, see the great lake, observe the rivers and what tribes lived in that region, while at the same time he might explore the mines and the rarest things amongst the tribes in those parts, so that on his return we might be informed of the truth thereof. We asked him if this would be agreeable to him; for it was not my wish to force him, but so soon as the request was made, he accepted the journey with great willingness.

Iroquot was delighted to take Brûlé home with him for the winter, and treat him as his own son, but the other chiefs refused; if the lad fell sick, or suffered an accident, wouldn't the French make war on them? They proposed that, in exchange, Champlain take a Wendat boy with him to France to report on all the fine things he would see there: both boys would be returned to the Richelieu River rendezvous the next June. Champlain and the chosen youth, renamed Savignon, agreed.

"We separated with many protestations of friendship" Champlain writes. "They went off in the direction of the great rapid of the river of Canada, and I went back to Québec."

Paddling and portaging a birchbark canoe above the tumultuous Lachine Rapids, Étienne Brûlé entered a world no European had seen. To evade the Iroquois, who controlled Lake Ontario, the canoe brigade, laden with French cloth, knives, axes and beads, took an arduous northern route to Lake Huron up the Ottawa River. Among the river's many rapids Brûlé observed a ceremony that left a deep impression on his imagination; he mentioned it thirteen years later to a gossipy Recollet missionary, Brother Gabriel Sagard. Sagard describes it in a discussion of spiritual beliefs in his memoir, *A Long Journey to the Country of the Huron:*

They believe that there are certain spirits which bear rule over one place, and others over another, some over rivers, others over journeying, trading, warfare, feasts and diseases, and many other matters. Some-times they offer them tobacco and make some kind of prayer and ritual observance to obtain from them what they desire. They also showed me many mighty rocks on the way to Québec, in which they believed a spirit lived and ruled, and among others they showed me one which had something like a head and two upraised arms, and in the belly or middle of this mighty rock there was a deep cavern very difficult to approach. They tried to persuade me and make me believe absolutely, as they did, that this rock had been a mortal man like ourselves and that while lifting up his arms and hands he had been transformed into this stone and in course of time had become a mighty rock, to which they pay respect and offer tobacco when passing it in their canoes, not always, but when they are in doubt of a successful issue to their journey. And as they offer the tobacco, which they throw into the water against the rock itself, they say to it, 'Here, take courage, and let us have a good journey,' together with some other speech that I did not understand. The interpreter [Brûlé] assured us that he had once made a similar offering with them (for which we rebuked him sharply) and that the journey brought him more profit than any other he had ever made in those parts.

CATHOLIC OR PROTESTANT, Étienne Brûlé was no more or less religious than any other bright French teenager, and when it came to cruelty, Europeans, too, tortured their prisoners to death and burned heretics alive at the stake. A hostage, a spy, and a white-skinned freak,

In an imaginative interpretation by Rex Woods, Champlain bids Brûlé farewell; travelling with Algonquin and Wendat hunters and warriors, the young French-man became the first European to set eyes on what is now Ontario.

Brûlé chose to blend in with his adoptive family. He likely found Iroquet's crowded bark wigwam warmer in winter than Champlain's crude barracks at Québec, and the family's meals of whitefish, venison, pumpkin and corn soup, healthier and tastier. Admiring women and girls sewed him moccasins, and oiled his skin and hair with soft hands. Special occasions, and Brûlé's arrival would have been among them, were celebrated by feasts that rivalled a French carnival.

Brother Gabriel describes the variety of fashion and adornment:

The Algonquin women and girls divide their long hair into three parts, two hanging at the sides over their ears and along their cheeks, the other arranged behind in a plait, like a hammer hanging down and resting on their back. But the women of the Hurons and Petuns make only one tress of all their hair, which also lies on their back, tied and done up with

... leather thongs. As to the men, they have two great rolls like moustaches above their ears, and some of them only one, which they quite often twist and cord with feathers and other trifles. The rest of their hair is kept short, or else cut in sections, or with a ruff, or in any other way they please.

As a rule all the [native people], and especially the women and girls, are very careful to oil their hair, and the men to paint their faces and the rest of their

Canada Post celebrated the accomplishments of Étienne Brûlé with a stamp that was issued in March 1987.

BRÛLÉ APPROCHE DU LAC SUPÉRIEUR / BRÛLÉ NEARS LAKE SUPERIOR

body, when they are to take part in some feast or in public meetings; and if they have painted ornaments and wampum they do not forget them any more than glass beads, chaplets, and other trifles that the French use for trading with them. Their wampum is strung in different ways, some of it to make

necklaces three or four fingers in breadth, with all its threads covered up and inserted in the pieces of shell. The circumference of these necklaces is about three and a half feet or more, and the women put many of them on their necks, according to their means and wealth. Then they have others, strung like our rosaries, fastened to their ears and hanging down, and chains of the same wampum which they fasten to both hips, and these are arranged in front in a slant over their thighs or the girdles they wear. Some of them have also belts and other finery made porcupine quills dyed crimson red and very neatly interwoven.

The young men are as much concerned to dress themselves up and put on paint as the girls. They oil their hair, stick feathers in it, while some make themselves little ruffs of down to put around their neck. Some have frontlets of snake-skin the tails of which hang behind. They paint their body and face in various colors, black, green, red, violet, and in many other ways. Others have their body and face marked in divisions, with representations of snakes, lizards, squirrels and other animals, and chiefly those of the Tobacco nation [Petun] who, almost all, have their bodies thus patterned. It makes them frightful and hideous to those unaccustomed to it.

If celibate Sagard could not take his eyes off this sensual pageantry, how could young Brûlé resist seduction? Among the Wendat, sex was open, casual and unabashed. Young women commonly had several partners until they became pregnant; then they married the man they favored, or who pleased their parents.

When Brûlé was joyfully reunited with Champlain at the Richelieu River in June 1611, he was conversant in both the Wendat and Algonquin languages and had triumphantly run the treacherous Lachine Rapids. Champlain noted, however, with a hint of disapproval, that Brûlé was "dressed in the costume of the [Huron]".

Not surprisingly, the Wendat lad, Savignon, was dressed as a Frenchman. He spoke positively about his year in France, where he had been baptized, presented at court and sent to school, but he was eager to go home. The successful exchange, followed by days and nights of feasting, gift giving and negotiations, cemented an alliance between Champlain and the Lake Huron tribes that was both military and mercantile: in return for French aid in their wars with the Iroquois, the Wendat and Algonquin tribes would boycott the swarms of free traders on the St. Lawrence River and deal exclusively with Champlain's company. Étienne Brûlé returned to Huronia with Savignon, more as Champlain's agent and ambassador than his servant or "boy". For the next four years, Brûlé was the only European resident on the Great Lakes.

It was a time of prosperity and peace. Huronia's fortified towns and satellite hamlets, surrounded by thousands of acres of cultivated fields, housed an estimated 20,000 people. French tools and brass kettles were improving their stan-

dard of living; since the French refused to give them fire-arms, warriors used sharpened scrap metal instead of stone to tip their arrows, and fashioned swords into spears.

They were spoiling for a fight. After the last of the Wendat and Petun had moved from the Lake Ontario watershed to the shores of Lake Huron forty or more years earlier, their former homeland became a no man's land, their ancestral Carrying Place, or portage, a warpath used by enemy Iroquois raiding parties. Now that the Iroquois, enticed by English and Dutch traders on the Hudson River, were turning their attention to the east, the Wendat were growing cocky.

On August 1, 1615, Champlain, with a dozen or so Frenchmen, arrived in Huronia to accompany an army of warriors on a foray into the heart of Iroquois territory. The warriors' ritual dancing and feasting lasted nearly a month, while Champlain, touring all the villages, was treated as royally as the King of France. On September 1, the war party began to gather at the narrows between Lake Couchiching and the broader lake they called Taronto (which we now know as Lake Simcoe). Their goal was an Iroquois stronghold several days' march inland from the southeastern shore of Lake Ontario (most likely near the Oneida River in today's New York State), and they hoped to be joined by warriors from the southern allies of the Wendat and Algonquin, the Susquehannock.

"When all were assembled, with their weapons, meal and necessaries," Champlain records in his journal, "they decided to select the most resolute men in order to go and give notice of our departure to those who were to assist us with five hundred men, so that these might join us at the right time before the enemy's fortress. They dispatched two canoes with twelve of the most stalwart [Huron], and by the same means one of our interpreters who asked me to let him make this journey, to which I readily agreed, since he was drawn thereto of his own inclination, and by this means would see their country and could observe the tribes that inhabit it. The danger was not small, inasmuch as it was necessary to pass through the midst of the enemy."

Étienne Brûlé was the interpreter, and on September 8, 1615, he and his twelve companions paddled off to meet their allies on the headwaters of the Susquehanna River. Their exact route is unknown, but they were in a hurry – Champlain had scheduled the attack on the Iroquois fortress for October 11 – and their shortest, most familiar path was down Lake Taronto (Simcoe) to the Toronto Carrying Place, then across Lake Ontario or the Niagara River to make a long detour on foot south of the enemy's strongholds on the Finger Lakes.

Champlain and the war party travelled southeast along the Trent River system to the Bay of Quinte. Brûlé and Champlain did not meet again for almost three years.

Brûlé's adventures, as he told them to Champlain, sound like tales from the Arabian Nights.

He and his companions made their way to the Susquehannock "by traversing woods, forests and dense and difficult thickets, and by marshy swamps, frightful and unfrequented places and wastes, all to avoid the danger of an encounter with their enemies."

They arrived in good time at the Susquehannocks' chief town, Carantouan, with two enemy Seneca they had taken prisoner after killing four others. However, the festivities that greeted their arrival were followed by lengthy deliberations, and the warriors, surprised by the unexpected invitation, were slow to assemble. By the time the Susquehannock war party reached the Iroquois fortress, only a three-day march to the north, they found no Frenchmen and no Huron/Algonquin army. They turned around and went home.

They had missed the battle by two days. Arriving eight days earlier, on October 10, Champlain had laid siege to the Iroquois town in the European manner, and tried to breach or destroy its thick wooden walls by setting them on fire; the Iroquois doused the fires by pouring water from gutters running along the tops of the walls. French musketeers, mounted on platforms, fired volleys into the compound; the Iroquois responded with showers of arrows. After six days of noisy, chaotic attacks that failed to flush the Iroquois from their impregnable stronghold, the besieging army retreated, carrying their wounded, Champlain among them, in wicker baskets. Champlain, disabled by a painful arrow wound in his knee,

Etienne Brûlé's last lap of the Portage to Lake Ontario 1615

The final leg of Brûlé's 1615 journey west to Lake Ontario.

was no longer the invincible "man of iron".

Brûlé spent the winter with the Susquehannock. He told Champlain of travelling down a river to the sea, past islands and coasts inhabited by powerful, warlike tribes, where the winter was so mild that snow melted on reaching the ground. Returning to Huronia through enemy territory in the spring, Brûlé and his guides escaped a Seneca ambush by fleeing into the woods. Champlain writes:

Brûlé got so separated from the others that he could no longer retrace his steps nor find the trail, and thus he continued to wander through the woods and forests for some days without eating and almost despairing of his life from pressure of hunger. At last he came by chance upon a little path which he determined to follow no matter where it might lead, were it towards the enemy or not, preferring to place himself in their hands through the trust he had in God, than to die alone so miserably; moreover, he knew how to speak their language, and this might bring some advantage to him.

Now he had not proceeded far when he discovered three [men], laden with fish, who were returning to their village. He made haste to run after them to join them, and coming near them he began to call out to them as is their custom, at which call they turned around and, in fear and apprehension, prepared to flee and leave their burden, but Brûlé, speaking to them, reassured them and made them

Lost and increasingly desperate, Brûlé wandered for days through a heavily forested landscape, much like this one, south of Lake Ontario.

lay down their bows and arrows in token of peace, and likewise Brûlé laid down his arms. And on coming up with them, after having made them hear his mishap and the wretched state to which he was reduced, they smoked together, as is their custom when they and their acquaintances visit one another.

Brûlé's new friends took him to their village, where, surrounded by an angry mob, he was closely questioned by a chief: Was he not one of the French nation who were making war on them? Champlain continues:

Thereupon he made reply that he belonged to another better nation that was desirous only of their acquaintance and friendship, which they refused to believe, and rushed upon him, and tore out his nails with their teeth, burned him with red-hot firebrands, plucked out his beard hair by hair, contrary nevertheless to the wish of their chief. One of them spied an Agnus Dei which he had hung about his neck, and tried to seize it and tear it off, but Brûlé said to him (in a resolute voice): 'If you take it and put me to death, you shall see that immediately afterwards you and all your house will die suddenly'; to which the savage paid no attention, but pursuing his evil purpose tried to seize the Agnus Dei and tear it from him; and altogether were prepared to put him to death, after first making him suffer many pains and tortures. But God who had mercy on him would not permit it, but in His providence caused the sky which had been clear and fine suddenly to become overcast and to be filled with thick heavy clouds, which ended in thunder and lightning so violent and continuous as to be something strange and awful.

The crowd scattered. The chief unbound Brûlé, took him into his lodge, doctored his injuries and welcomed him as an honored guest. Adopting the role of ambassador, Brûlé promised, on his return to Huronia, to make a lasting peace between the Seneca, the Wendat/Huron and the French. His diplomacy worked; after a long visit, Seneca scouts saw him safely on his homeward path.

Brûlé may have framed his salvation story – dying hero saved by divine thunderbolt – to suit his listeners, but it reveals the ambiguity of his situation. After six years living among native North Americans, he was instantly recognized as French; he had a beard and wore a Catholic medal around his neck. Were his eyes blue, his skin freckled and his hair blond or red? With no blood relations among the Wendat, Brûlé was an outsider, yet while he acted an agent and explorer for the French, he seems to have had no edcation in navigation or map making; nobody knows to this day which river he followed to the Atlantic Ocean. Still, at great risk to his own life, he had seen more of North America and its inhabitants than any other European. Champlain praised Brûlé's work, and promised him rich rewards, but there is no evidence that he was given a seigneury at Québec, an audience with King Louis XIII, or that he was paid his salary of 100 pistoles a year. Discovering that the Freshwater Sea, La Mer Douce, as Champlain called Lake Huron, was not the Pacific Ocean, Champlain lost interest in western exploration and turned his energies towards building a colony at Québec.

Cast adrift, Brûlé became a fur trader, the first Canadian *coureur de bois*. By 1623, he was no longer the only Frenchman in Huronia. That autumn, two Recollet priests, Joseph Le Caron and Nicolas Viel and Brother Gabriel Sagard, arrived to start a mission; with them, instead of the French settlers Champlain had promised, came a dozen young men to act as guards and laborers. Le Caron, who had wintered here with Champlain seven years before, wanted to teach the Wendat and Algonquin the French language, manners and morals before their baptism into the Catholic faith, yet he insisted that the Recollets live apart in their own bark house. Although they wore simple gray robes and went barefoot, their isolation, chastity, prayers, chants, and vessels of gold and silver, confirmed to the Wendat that they were wizards with supernatural powers, just like their own medicine men; wasn't the priests' wooden cross a tree?

A SPIRITUAL PEOPLE, the Wendat were not averse to welcoming a benign new god into their pantheon, and their sorcerers, as the Recollets called them, eagerly invited their French colleagues to witness their healing ceremonies and discuss theology. "They have some respect for those spirits which they call Oki," Brother Gabriel observed, "but this word Oki means a great devil just as much as a great angel, a raging devilish disposition as well as a great, wise, understanding, or efficient intelligence, which does and knows something out of the ordinary. They also give the name Oki to their medicine men and magicians … even to persons who are mad, infuriated, possessed of the devil."

Roman Catholic and Wendat beliefs, with their saints, devils, miracles and cults of the dead, might have been compatible had the Recollets not insisted on obedience, discipline, corporal punishment and sexual inhibition as conditions for salvation. By the priests' bourgeois standards, the Huron were crude, ignorant and licentious; *"huron"* was French slang for a "rough, uncultured bumpkin". Even sociable Sagard, who cheerfully conversed with the villagers in pantomime, complained about their simple diet of cornmeal mush, boiled without salt, herbs or spices, with only an occasional fish, bones, scales, entrails and all, added for flavor. And, *quelle horreur,* no wine! The Wendat did not make beer, wine or spirits, and French traders did not give them brandy; the Recollets soon learned to make their own wine out of wild grapes. Meat, preferably dog or bear, was reserved for community feasts, debaucheries the fastidious friars refused to attend.

ETIENNE BRULE
BORN IN FRANCE IN 1595, ARRIVED IN QUEBEC IN 1608,
WITH A GENIUS FOR EXPLORATION BRULE FROM LAKE
HURON THENCE TO LAKE SIMCOE AND SOUTHWARD
MADE THE HUMBER HIS ROUTE TO LAKE ONTARIO IN 1615
— THIS TABLET —
COMMEMORATES HIS JOURNEY OF DISCOVERY BY THE
PATHWAY OF THE HUMBER, AND HONORS THE NAME OF
ETIENNE BRULE THE FIRST WHITE MAN TO SEE LAKE ONTARIO

Though Brûlé's accomplishments may not have been rewarded by Champlain, modern historians have pieced together his contributions and history buffs have recognized them. Among the latter was William Hodgson, who created this plaque to adorn his Old Mill Restaurant (now the Old Mill Inn and Spa), created on the site of John Simcoe's King's Mill, which was built on the Humber River in 1794.

Not so Étienne Brûlé and the other young Frenchmen; they ate, danced and made love, according to the custom of the country. Yet Sagard, struggling to compile a dictionary of the Wendat/Huron language, befriended the interpreter. He recorded this conversation: "Brulé assured us that beyond the Freshwater Sea [Lake Huron] there was another very large lake which empties into it by a waterfall, which has been called Saut de Gaston, of a width of almost two leagues; which lake and the Freshwater Sea have almost thirty days' journey by canoe in length, according to the account of the [native people]; but, according to the interpreter's account, they are four hundred leagues in length."

Brûlé and a French companion, Grenole, seem to have been the first Europeans to reach Sault Ste. Marie and Lake Superior; Brûlé's estimate of the size of Lake Superior, and a bar of copper he produced, suggest that he travelled a considerable distance along the lake's shores. At the rapids, the Frenchmen would have met a powerful Algonquin nation, the Ojibwe, who controlled access to Lake Superior's riches. In the summer of 1624, Sagard, returning to Québec for provisions, accepted Brûlé's invitation to accompany his canoes as the Wendat embarked on their annual trading expedition down the Ottawa River to the St. Lawrence.

Camped with the Algonquin at the mouth of the Richelieu River and waiting for the French traders to arrive, Sagard became impatient to get to Québec: "I decided to have our canoe launched, and I did so at break of day when all … were still asleep, and I wakened no one except the interpreter, to follow me if he could. He did so immediately and we made such speed, aided by the current, and there being no rapid to get past, that we made twenty-four full leagues that day in spite of the discomfort of rain."

Champlain tells us how Sagard repaid Brûlé's kindness:

On the sixteenth, Brother Gabriel arrived with seven canoes, to our great joy. He told us all that had happened during the winter … and the bad life which most of the Frenchmen had led in the country of the Hurons; amongst others the interpreter Brûlé. And the influence of example was very bad in sending out such evil-livers, who ought instead to have been severely chastised; for this man was recognized as being vicious in character, and much addicted to women.

THE DEMONIZATION of Brûlé and the other young Frenchmen Champlain had assigned to live among the northern Algonquin reflected a power struggle in the French court between the old merchant traders, who saw the native peoples as entrepreneurs and customers, and pious imperialists intent on establishing New France as a Roman Catholic agricultural colony. The imperialists won; in 1625, Brûlé and his fellow interpreter/agent/adventurers in the hinterland were given the option of returning to France or settling on farms on the lower St. Lawrence.

Brûlé chose Paris. He was welcomed by the new owners of the trading monopoly, the Company of One Hundred Associates, and assigned to act as an escort to a baptized Wendat youth, Amantacha, who was returning to his family after two years in a French school; Brûlé may have known Amantacha all the boy's life. They sailed in the spring of 1628 with a fleet of four French merchant ships carrying 400 settlers, their possessions, and a year's provisions for Champlain's impoverished little habitation at Québec. It was a risky venture. Charles I of England, miffed at France's tardiness in paying his royal bride's dowry, had declared war, and commissioned an English merchant, Gervase Kirke, to kick the French company out of Canada. By the time the French supply ships lumbered into the Gulf of St. Lawrence, Kirke's three privateers, commanded by his oldest son, David, had captured the French outpost at Tadoussac and demanded that Champlain surrender Québec; Champlain boldly refused.

Unwilling to attempt an armed assault, Kirke was retreating downriver when he spied the French ships off Gaspé, captured them without bloodshed, and sailed them to England. The captives were returned to France except Amantacha, who was paraded about London as the son of the "King of Canada", and his guardian, Brûlé, along with a few defectors.

Whether Brûlé willingly joined the English cause, or was compelled, he and Amantacha sailed with the Kirkes on their second, successful blockade of Québec in the summer of 1629. With its inhabitants facing starvation, and no French ships in sight, Champlain surrendered without a fight on July 19. Enraged at seeing Brûlé and another of his protégés, Nicolas Marsolet, among the victorious English, Champlain denounced them as traitors and infidels, threatening: "God will punish you if you do not mend your ways. You are losing your honour; you will be pointed at with scorn on all sides, wherever you may be. Better it would be for you to die than to live in the world under such conditions … if you are caught, you who are obliged to move about so much, you run a great risk of being seized and punished."

Five days later, sailing back to England with captive Champlain and all the French priests, the Kirkes encountered French supply ships in the Gulf of St. Lawrence. After exchanging gunfire, the French managed to convey the information that France and England had signed a peace treaty three months earlier: Québec would be given back to the French.

Étienne Brûlé returned, with Amantacha, to the only home he knew, Huronia, and settled in the village of Toanché near Georgian Bay. We hear no more of him until the summer of 1633, when frightened Wendat traders brought news of his violent death to Québec. Weeks earlier, Brûlé had been murdered by the people he had lived among for more than twenty years. Champlain reassured

The Grand Royal Coat of Arms of France and Navarre symbolized the French monarchy for 200 years, from 1589–1790.

their spokesman, Amantacha, of France's continued friendship; Brûlé, he said, was no longer considered French since he had gone to the English.

The first Frenchman to reach the crime scene was the Jesuit priest, Jean de Brébeuf. Deported to France by the Kirkes after the surrender of Québec, Brébeuf had returned to his Toanché mission in August 1634, in the midst of an epidemic he describes as "a violent fever, sort of measles or smallpox". Abandoned by his canoemen on the lakeshore, Brébeuf writes, "I set out to find our village, which fortunately I came upon at about three-quarters of a league – having seen with tenderness and emotion as I passed along, the place where we had lived and celebrated the Holy sacrifice of the Mass during three years now turned into a fine field; and also the site of the old village where, except for one cabin, nothing remained but the ruins of the others. I saw likewise the spot where poor Estienne Brûlé was barbarously and traitorously murdered."

The Wendat had torched Toanché and built two new villages, a community divided. They told Brébeuf, "The Algonquains and even the Huron of the other villages threatened us with death if we went there [to Québec] on account of the murder of Brûlé," and that Champlain had demanded "four heads" as reparation for their crime. Only Brother Gabriel Sagard, writing later from hearsay, claimed that Brûlé had been "eaten by the Huron", but they felt so guilty many believed that Brûlé's enraged sister had sent the epidemic to annihilate them.

The murderers almost certainly were Aouandoïé, the wealthy chieftain Brébeuf was lodging with, and his clansman, Aenons. In 1636, preparing for a Feast of the Dead, a delegation of Wendat asked the Jesuits' permission to disinter Brûlé's body from its grave in the woods, and mingle his bones with their own dead in a common ossuary. The Jesuits refused, insisting that Brûlé and the corpse of another Frenchman, Guillaume Chaudron, must be buried in consecrated ground. In the angry squabble that ensued, Brébeuf writes that Aenons stepped forward and claimed Brûlé's body, stating that "he had embarked him and brought him to this country." A loud whisper went around the lodge: Oh yes! Aenons was entitled to Brûlé's body since he had killed him! Aenons rejected the body, and the Jesuits, anxious to keep the peace, let the issue drop

Brûlé seems to have been the victim of a clan power struggle. Aouandoïé and Aenons were members of the Huron/Algonquin oligarchy that controlled the Georgian Bay fishery and the lucrative Ottawa River trade route; an attempt by Brûlé to make peace with the enemy Seneca, as promised, would have diverted Lake Huron trade down the Toronto Carrying Place to Lake Ontario, a safer, faster journey to the St. Lawrence River. Clever, brave, multilingual, with contacts from Lake Superior and the Susquehanna River to the salons of Paris and London, Brûlé, in his prime, would have been poised to assume a position of authority in Wendat society, a prospect intolerable to some.

This map of New France, created in 1641, makes it clear how much of North America was still a mystery to the French.

At times and in some places, as here on a dark winter day, the Humber River speaks of its grim past.

The Demise
of the
Wendat

Father Jean de Brébeuf's arrival

among the Wendat (or "Huron", as he knew them)

with two other priests and some French workmen,

coincided with, or perhaps precipitated,

a series of devastating epidemics.

Brass Jesuit rings from Colonial Michilimackinac.

IN 1636 AND 1637, influenza swept through the longhouses, followed the next year by a virulent fever; in 1639, smallpox killed thousands. Within six years, almost all the Wendat or Huron had fallen ill, and half, likely more, had died. The French, on the other hand, had survived. The Wendat blamed the strange clothing, food and religious paraphernalia the Jesuits had imported, rightly guessing that invisible evil spirits – or viruses, as we now know them – had travelled on ships from Europe and spread throughout the nations of the St. Lawrence watershed. Since only a few native North Americans had ever mingled with the French on the St. Lawrence, the rest of the population had no immunity.

The loss of so many women meant crops went unplanted or were left to rot in the fields; children were motherless, and bereaved men hungry, angry and sorrowful. When all the villagers' medicines, prayers and rituals failed to cure these diseases, they accused the Jesuits of annihilating them by witchcraft.

It was true that the Catholic missionaries had intended to destroy the Wendat religion and culture, though not the people themselves. Yet as the Jesuits tended the sick and, often surreptitiously, baptized the dying, the exotic medicines they offered, such as raisins and sugar, were interpreted as poisons, and baptism was deemed a charm to hasten death. Painted images of the saints, Christ and the Virgin Mary embodied powerful spirits, while communion was taken literally; the Jesuits were eating a corpse. The priests refused to be driven away by threats to kill them; firm in their faith in God, they let it be known that they rejoiced in suffering and welcomed martyrdom. The Wendat held back, fearing that if any harm came to their dangerous black-robed guests, the French would terminate their trading partnership.

Instead, the warriors turned their frustration and fury on the Iroquois, who, suffering from the same plagues, reciprocated; the Iroquois tortured and murdered Isaac Jogues, the only Jesuit they could get their hands on. North of Lake Ontario, the pathways and river valleys, prime hunting and fishing grounds, became bloody battlefields as rival war parties ambushed, kidnapped and killed each other. Battles were sometimes fought on the lake. In the summer of 1640, Wendat raiders paddling south encountered a flotilla of Iroquois canoes heading north; according to the *Jesuit Relations*, a Christian member of the culture, Ahatsistari, "jumped, alone and quite naked, into a large Canoe full of Foes, split open the head of the first one that he met, threw two others into the water, into which he himself leaped, upsetting the Canoe and all who were in it. Then, swimming with one hand, he killed and massacred with the other all who came near him." His companions captured the fleeing Iroquois and brought them back in triumph.

The Jesuits responded to the terror by congregating in their own fortified compound, Ste. Marie-aux-Hurons, on the Wye River. Enclosed by a palisade, the settlement included a chapel, timber houses for the priests, barracks and shops for their workmen, a cookhouse, a barn, and, on the outskirts, a hospital, a church, bark houses for native visitors and a Christian cemetery. This chaste little French community grew its own corn and vegetables, made wine from wild grapes and raised French cattle. It also symbolized a cultural chasm between the Jesuits and the people of the region. Spiritually, their beliefs were similar enough that many Wendat readily accepted Christianity, not realizing that prayers to these new gods were not enough, at least according to the Jesuit world view. The Jesuits also insisted that they must renounce all other gods, including feasts and healing ceremonies, cover their nakedness, refrain from sex until marriage, never divorce and whip their disobedient children. Most converts ignored these inexplicable, impossible rules; when they did not, their aberrant social behavior incited quarrels and suspicions of witchcraft. Even in the afterlife, Christians went to a heaven that did not include their ancestors, while the unconverted went to hell. The result was families that broke apart and Christian men and women who were shunned or murdered by pagan relatives.

For their part, the priests – most of them, like Brébeuf, the sons of minor gentry or respectable bourgeoisie – abhorred the uninhibited squalor of longhouse life. Even Champlain, a

Ameriq. Sept.   L'An 1801.   Possession Anglaises.

J.G.S.Sauveur Del.   Mixelle j. Sculp.

Homme & Femme Iroquois

roughened soldier and seaman, complained about the fleas and the mice. Father Jérôme Lalemant, founder of Ste. Marie, writes of the Wendat/Huron: "If you go to visit them in their cabins – and you must go there oftener than once a day – you will find there a miniature picture of Hell – seeing nothing ordinarily but fire and smoke, and on every side naked bodies, black and half roasted, mingled pell-mell with the dogs, which are held as dear as the children of the house, and share the beds, plates and food of their masters. Everything is in a cloud of dust, and, if you go within, you will not reach the end of the cabin before you are completely befouled with soot, filth and dirt." For priests like Lalement, a Christian life required privacy, quiet, and a bed with clean linen.

The priests' vivid observations of Aboriginal life, published in France as the *Jesuit Relations,* also tell the gruesome story of a ferocious, relentless Iroquois assault on the heart of the Wendat/Huron nation. Using the Toronto Carrying Place as their war road, in 1643, a band of Iroquois attacked and burned a Wendat village, killing and carrying away almost all its inhabitants; by 1645, Iroquois war canoes controlled Lake Simcoe, driving the residents from their fishing camps and kidnapping women near the village of Contarea on the lake's northwest shore.

"At the beginning of Spring," the *Relations* tells, "a band of Iroquois – having landed near one of our frontier villages, by favour of a very dark night, and having concealed itself in the woods – surrounded a company of women who were just going out for work in the fields, and so quickly carried them off in their canoes, that two hundred men in arms, who ran up at their first cries, could not arrive soon enough to save one of them, but were only in time to witness the sad tears of their wives, their mothers and their children who were taken captive."

IN 1647, the Wendat abandoned Contarea, once a major centre, and all their other encampments near Lake Simcoe. The loss of the Contarea corn-fields and the fishery at the Couchiching Narrows raised the spectre of famine, and the forests were full of marauding Iroquois who ambushed un-wary hemp gatherers and deer hunters; the Jesuits tell of seeing escaped prisoners with burns and mutilated hands. Wendat warriors, unable to drive the Iroquois away, were captured by the hundreds, and their villages were left undefended. At dawn on July 4, 1648, the Iroquois stormed into Teanaostaiaé [St. Joseph], a well-fortified town of about 2,000 in the Sturgeon Valley, just as Father Antoine Daniel had finished saying mass. In the melee, most of the women and children fled, but the Christians took refuge with Father Daniel in the church. When the Iroquois attacked the church, Father Daniel strode out to confront them; he died in a hail of arrows, a musket ball through his chest. His body was stripped, hacked and thrown into the burning church. The fate of

DRAWING FROM *CHAMPLAIN'S VOYAGES*, 1619

The Iroquois family, opposite, and other native North Americans whose portraits were painted between the mid-seven-teenth and early nine-teenth centuries were often protrayed in a classical, almost courtly fashion. And some, including Elizabeth Simcoe, found their manner of speaking "like that of Greek or Roman Orators" (see page 121).

Left: Champlain's drawing of a Wendat warrior shows him outfitted for the ritu-alized conflict of the early seventeenth century.

Above: Father Jean de Brébeuf

Opposite: Brébeuf and Gabriel Lalemant, along with their faithful Wendat converts from the village of St. Louis, were captured; the priests were tortured by the Iroquois.

his parishioners is unknown, but after torching the longhouses, the Iroquois departed with as many as 700 prisoners.

The Iroquois were now an occupying army, with 1,000 warriors camped in the woods south of Lake Simcoe. Early in the spring of 1649, they set out on foot to destroy the Jesuit missions on Georgian Bay. Before dawn on March 16, the Iroquois silently infiltrated the half-deserted, unguarded village of Taenhatentaron and took the sleeping people captive. Taenhatentaron then became the base camp for their final assault on St. Louis and the stronghold of Ste. Marie. Warned of the impending attack, the residents of St. Louis fled, leaving to defend the mission only eighty warriors. Two Jesuit priests, Jean de Brébeuf and Gabriel Lalemant, chose to stand with their Christian soldiers. After two failed assaults, the Iroquois overran and burned the village. Brébeuf, Lalemant and the surviving warriors were led back to Taenhatentaron to be tortured. The priests were stripped, beaten, tied to stakes, burned and mutilated; Brébeuf died that afternoon, Lalemant the next morning.

This grisly distraction gave Christian Wendat/Huron refugees at Ste. Marie time to regroup; supported by a few French soldiers, they beat off the Iroquois and recaptured the ruins of St. Louis. Their victory was brief, however. The Iroquois retook St. Louis the next day, but with casualties so high they decided to retreat; on March 19, they marched away south to Lake Ontario, and home, driving before them their cavalcade of prisoners.

Leaderless and defenceless, the Wendat burned their remaining villages, abandoned their fields and scattered into small family groups, hiding in the forest or seeking refuge with distant kin and clans. In June, the Jesuits rafted their food, cattle and possessions to Gahoendoe Island off the Penetanguishene Peninsula and burned Ste. Marie-aux-Hurons.

The destruction of the Wendat/Huron confederacy in Southern Ontario was total and final. The Iroquois did not rebuild the villages or cultivate the fields in Huronia and the region reverted to wilderness. Why, after centuries of ritualized raiding, had the Iroquois decided to exterminate their northern cousins, and how had they achieved such a swift, decisive victory? Apart from hunting deer and beaver, the Iroquois did not take advantage of the territory they had gained, and they didn't need to wrest the Great Lakes fur trade from the Algonquin, since they regularly plundered their canoe brigades on the St. Lawrence River. They had English guns – the French gave muskets only to Christian warriors – but guns were heavy, hard to reload and useless in stealthy woodland warfare. Both the Wendat and Iroquois had been debilitated by epidemics; the Iroquois may have suffered less, and wanted captives to replenish their population, but how could they muster such an overwhelming armed force?

In *The Children of Aataentsic: A History of the Huron People to 1660*, anthropologist Bruce

Trigger offers a provocative insight. Describing the torture of Brébeuf and Lalemant, he writes: "Many Huron were present who in the past had been taken prisoner by the Iroquois and been adopted by them. [They] played a leading role in torturing the Jesuits, whom they regarded as sorcerers responsible for the ruin of their homeland. In addition to the usual torments, the Huron amused themselves by repeatedly pouring boiling water over the priests in a mockery of baptism. These prisoners must all have had relatives still living in the Huron country, whom they were anxious to rescue as the Huron confederacy collapsed."

The prominent role played by these collaborators may explain the unusual ease with which the invaders were able to infiltrate palisaded villages, for their relatives inside seem to have assisted them. The *Relations* tell of village watchmen falling asleep, and defenders too slow or too fearful to pursue kidnappers. Villages and fields were abandoned without a struggle. War parties were surprised, surrounded and captured. Had they lost courage, or did they willingly join the Iroquois? Faced with the choice of being Christian or Iroquois, militant Wendat "traditionalists", as Trigger calls them, chose to be Iroquois.

It wasn't hard to do, for many had relatives among the Seneca. Seneca women and children had been captured and adopted by the Wendat for untold generations, as Wendat captives had become Seneca. They were both agricultural peoples with shared spiritual beliefs who spoke dialects of a common language, and there were practical reasons for their interrelationships. The Wendat, confined to their peninsula, were running short of arable land, and without corn to trade they would become impoverished; the powerful Iroquois confederacy, meanwhile, was poised to push west and south into the fertile Lake Erie basin and the Ohio Valley. The Wendat/Huron culture appears to have been destroyed not by invasion, but by a revolutionary civil war.

If the war's purpose had been to drive the Christians out of Huronia, it succeeded. So many destitute Huron converts gathered around the new Jesuit mission on Gahoendoe [Christian] Island, the priests could not feed and clothe them during the winter; living on acorns, offal and, in extremity, disinterred corpses, they died of cold and starvation. In the spring of 1650, the Jesuits abandoned the island and, with some 300 faithful, retreated to Québec.

Traditional villagers relocated among the Petun and the Neutral, or moved in with their Algonquin neighbours around Lake Huron. The most visionary refugees cleared fields on the west shore of Lake Michigan, and traded corn for furs and fish with the Odawa and Ojibwe, who controlled the hub of the Great Lakes, the Straits of Michilimackinac. The Iroquois did not entirely leave Ontario, however. Instead, they built fortified villages at the mouths of the Trent, Rouge and Humber Rivers to protect their pathways to the north. Before long the French would return.

The gardens, at left, and entrance, inset, at Sainte-Marie among the Hurons, in Midland, Ontario. The recreated seventeenth-century Jesuit mission offers educational programs, self-guided visits and guided tours focusing on a crucial period in the region's long history.

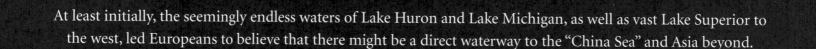

At least initially, the seemingly endless waters of Lake Huron and Lake Michigan, as well as vast Lake Superior to the west, led Europeans to believe that there might be a direct waterway to the "China Sea" and Asia beyond.

The Search
for the
China Sea

"That very same year [1678],

on the Eighteenth of November, I took leave

of our Monks at Fort Frontenac, and after mutual

Embraces and Expressions of Brotherly

and Christian Charity, I embark'd

in a Brigantine of about ten Tuns."

THE WINDS and the Cold of the Autumn were then very violent, insomuch that our Crew was afraid to go into so little a Vessel. This oblig'd us and the Sieur de la Motte our Commander, to keep our course on the North-side of the Lake, to shelter our selves under the Coast, against the North-west Wind, which otherwise wou'd have forc'd us upon the Southern Coast of the Lake. The Voyage prov'd very difficult, because … Winter being near at hand.

On the 26th, we were in great danger about Two large Leagues off the Land, where we were oblig'd to lie at Anchor all that Night at sixty Fathom Water and above; but at length the Wind coming to the North-East, we sailed on, and arriv'd safely at the further end of Lake Ontario, call'd by the Iroquese, Skannadario. We came pretty near to one of their Villages call'd Tajajagon, lying about Seventy Leagues from Fort Frontenac or Catarokouy.

We barter'd some Indian Corn with the Iroquese, who could not sufficiently admire us, and came frequently to see us on board our Brigantine, which for our security, we had brought to an Anchor into a River, though before we could get in, we run a ground three times, which oblig'd us to put Fourteen Men into Canou's, and cast the Balast of our Ship over-board to get her off again. That River falls into the Lake; but for fear of being frozen up therin, we were forc'd to cut the Ice with Axes and other Instruments.
    – Father Louis Hennepin
       A New Discovery of a Vast Country
       in America

Artist John David Kelly imagines the reaction of people used to much smaller boats, on the first sighting of a large sailing ship on Lake Erie.

Hennepin, an adventurous Recollet priest, was the first European to record a visit, if unintended, to Teiaiagon, a palisaded village on a high, flat promontory above the mouth of the river the Iroquois called Toronto. The expedition's commander, Dominique La Motte de Lucière, was heading southwest to the Niagara River, where, on behalf of his business associate, René-Robert Cavelier de La Salle, he was to scout a site for a fort; it was to be the first French fort built on the Great Lakes west of Fort Frontenac, the seigneury and fur trading post given to La Salle by his patron, Louis de Buade, Comte de Frontenac, Governor of New France.

La Salle was not an army officer or an aristocrat; the Caveliers were a wealthy merchant family in Rouen, Normandy, with investments in the fur trade of New France. René-Robert had little money of his own. In 1660, at the age of seventeen, he had joined the Jesuits, and although he left the order amid hard feelings seven years later, his vow of poverty had excluded him from receiving any inheritances. He arrived in Québec in 1667 as a protégé of his older brother, Jean Cavelier, a priest with the mission of St. Sulpice on Montréal Island. The Sulpicians gave young La Salle a tract of land at the Lachine Rapids, expecting he would seize the opportunity to build a colony there, but within two years he had sold everything but his house. In July 1669, with a flotilla of nine canoes and two Sulpician priests, La Salle headed west across Lake Ontario

Though done long after his death, this drawing is purported to be a likeness of René-Robert Cavelier, Sieur de La Salle.

in search of the Ohio River, "the way to the Southern Sea, and thereby the route to China."

A fragile peace with the Iroquois had made it possible for the French to venture on to a lake they boldly renamed Lac Frontenac, and to attempt to pass through Seneca country southwest of the lake towards the Ohio River watershed. The Seneca, who had captured Étienne Brûlé in 1616, did not pull out La Salle's beard or fingernails, but, after weeks of evasiveness and empty rhetoric they politely guided the French to the north of the lake, toward the rivers they already knew.

Here, in a village near Burlington Bay, they had the good luck to meet Adrien Jolliet, a Canadian fur trader returning from an expedition to Lake Superior in search of copper mines. Jolliet told them of a possible river route to the Ohio through the country of the Odawa and Potawotomi tribes on the west shore of Lake Michigan. The priests were eager to winter among the Potawotomi, but La Salle, pleading a fever, turned back towards Montréal.

It was a dire mistake. Four years later, on June 15, 1673, Adrien's brother, Louis Jolliet, and a Jesuit missionary, Jacques Marquette, in two canoes with five voyageurs, reached the Mississippi River at the mouth of the Wisconsin River; their quick route to the Wisconsin had taken them up the Fox River from Green Bay on Lake Michigan to a short portage into the Mississippi watershed. Paddling with the current past the confluence of the Iowa, Missouri and Ohio rivers, they were welcomed by the numerous Illinois tribes until they reached the hostile Quapaws south of the Arkansas River. Perceiving signs of Spanish influence, and believing themselves to be much closer to the ocean than they were, the expedition turned back in late July; three months later they were safely back at the mission of Saint-François-Xavier on Green Bay.

IN FRANCE, Jolliet and Marquette's astonishing achievement was greeted with dismay; La Belle Rivière did not flow west to the ephemeral China Sea, but, alas, south towards the Gulf of Mexico and France's Spanish enemies. Jolliet had failed to locate the river's mouth and he had lost his maps and log books when his canoe upset in the St. Lawrence rapids on his return home; his three companions had drowned. When Jolliet was refused permission to establish a small colony in the land of the Illinois he had discovered, La Salle seized his opportunity. Embellishing Jolliet's stories of a western paradise abounding in fish and venison, with a mild climate, fertile soil, herds of wild cattle (bison) and native people of a "tractable and social disposition", La Salle petitioned Louis XIV for permission to locate, at his own expense, three colonies, in exchange for "seigniorial rights over all lands which he may discover and colonize within twenty years, and the government of all the country in question."

King Louis had already claimed for France all of North America from the Mississippi River to the New England colonies, from James Bay south to Mexico. This kingdom was unexplored, unmapped and undefended, but the Sun King wasn't going to allow a young bourgeois upstart to challenge his absolute authority; in May 1678, he gave La Salle five years to "labour at the discovery of the western parts of New France", in particular a route to Mexico, and to build all the forts he wished, as long as he did all this at his own expense, "and that you carry on no trade with the savages called Ottawas, or with other tribes who bring their peltries to Montreal."

It was a task designed to appeal to La Salle's

Created and signed at Versailles, France, in 1675, this document gave La Salle remarkable scope for discovery.

ambitious, restless nature; the Jesuits had called him *"inquietus"*. Impatient to achieve his first goal, a fort at the mouth of the Niagara River, La Salle launched his expedition across Lake Ontario in November 1678, in the teeth of winter blizzards. Contrary winds kept Father Hennepin's little brigantine trapped near Teiaiagon until December 5th; the next day they reached the Niagara River and the crew dragged the boat ashore below the thundering cataract that barred their way. The men built themselves bark wigwams on the frozen ground while La Motte and Hennepin parlayed with the suspicious Seneca. La Salle finally arrived on January 20, 1679, and he brought bad news; two canoe loads of the camp's winter provisions had

Building the *Griffon*, by Father Louis Hennepin. Though his style is clearly "Old World", it is clear that like a considerable number of early adventurers and priests, Hennepin had been trained as an artist.

been swept overboard when his own boat had foundered on the rocks near the river's mouth.

La Motte quit. He pleaded an inflammation of his eyes, but he may have taken fright at the task ahead: to build a ship of forty to sixty tons on the riverbank above Niagara Falls. La Salle's critics whispered that he was insane. How could he sail such a large vessel up roiling rapids, across uncharted lakes into unknown territory? The keel of the *Griffon*, as she was christened, was scarcely laid when La Salle departed for Fort Frontenac, travelling across the ice on foot, accompanied by two men and a dog sled, to bring fresh supplies. He left an Italian solider-of-fortune, Henri Tonty, in command of meddlesome Father Hennepin and a company of frightened, disillusioned shipwrights. Felling trees and sawing boards in the bitter cold, living on cornmeal mush and boiled whitefish, the men worked desperately to complete the *Griffon* as a fortress against the Seneca, who eyed this wooden monster with more hostility than the Trojans had the Greek invaders' horse. Urged on by Father Hennepin's Te Deums, the French carried over the steep rocky portage the ship's sails and rigging, five small cannon, boxes of muskets and ammunition, and an anchor so heavy it took four men, fortified with brandy, to carry it. As soon as the ice went out in the spring, they anchored the little ship in the stream and moved on board.

At the end of July, La Salle returned with more than a dozen men, including two more

Henri de Tonty by Nicolas Maes, 1677

Avantures mal-heureuses du Sieur de la Salle

Though its artist is unknown, this drawing is entitled "Loading the Griffon with its cargo of furs".

LIBRARY AND ARCHIVES CANADA / C-03180

Recollet priests and the ship's pilot. On August 7, 1679, amid the roaring of cannon and bellowed Te Deums, the *Griffon* set sail on Lake Erie. Easily negotiating the lake's shoals and sandbars, the ship sailed north up a narrow strait to a small lake La Salle named St. Clair, then reached Lake Huron on August 23. Tacking blindly towards Michilimackinac – the pilot had no idea where he was – the *Griffon* was caught in a violent storm. Hennepin records:

We brought down our Main Yards and Top-Mast, and let the Ship drive at the Mercy of the Wind, knowing no place to run to shelter our selves. M. la Salle, notwithstanding he was a Courageous Man, began to fear, and told us we were undone; and therefore every body fell upon is Knees to say his Prayers, and prepare himself for Death, except our Pilot, whom we could never oblige to pray; and he did nothing all that while but curse and swear against M. la Salle, who, as he said, had brought him thither to make him perish in a nasty Lake, and lose the Glory he had acquir'd by his long and happy Navigations on the Ocean.

On August 27, the *Griffon*, its cannon booming, arrived at Michilimackinac to a cacophonous welcome from the Wendat and Odawa who swarmed around the ship – the first on the Great Lakes – in their canoes. La Salle, draped in a scarlet cloak trimmed with gold lace, and accompanied by a honour guard of musketeers firing *feus de joie* into the air, paid ceremonial calls on the chiefs, while Henri Tonty went off to round up a group of Canadian *coureurs de bois* La Salle had sent to the Northwest to trade for furs the year before.

Early in September, the *Griffon* sailed into Lake Michigan. Here, La Salle's daring scheme reveals itself. By building a string of river forts south of the lake, he could evade the king's edict not to trade with the northern tribes by soliciting new customers among the Illinois and other populous southern nations. Using the *Griffon,* he would be able to transport a fortune in furs, hides and, with luck, Mexican gold, to Fort Frontenac along the quick new route he had found via Lake Erie and Lake Ontario.

After a profitable visit to the Potawatomi in Green Bay, the *Griffon* was already laden with furs. Why not send it back to Michilimackinac to pick up furs stored there, then home to Fort Niagara? In Montréal, La Salle's success would help persuade his anxious creditors that his enterprise was worth their support.

Giving no thought to the lateness of the season, the possibility that Fort Niagara – a crude warehouse – may have been burned by the Seneca, or the difficulty of portaging the *Griffon's* cargo around Niagara Falls to a ship that might not be there, La Salle dispatched his ship, with a crew of five, on its return journey; its captain was the bad-tempered pilot.

On September 19, La Salle, with fourteen men, including the three priests, paddled south

from Green Bay in four bark canoes loaded to the gunwales with trade goods, guns, carpenters' tools and a blacksmith's forge. On November 1, after numerous stops at lakeshore camps to make friends with startled natives, they built a small post at the mouth of the St. Joseph River. A month later, joined by Henri Tonty and twenty Frenchmen who had scouted the eastern shore of the

In any language, this is unmistakably Niagara Falls.

Created in 1688, this map of the Great Lakes and the southern reaches of New France demonstrates how France's knowledge of western North America had grown in less than a half-century.

lake, they paddled up the St. Joseph into a dreary landscape.

The natives had burned the prairies and vacated their villages for their winter hunting grounds. As the expedition paddled and portaged to the Illinois River on the Mississippi watershed, the men, disgruntled at more winter labour, lived on bear meat, stray bison and sacks of corn La Salle had liberated from a village storehouse. When they at last reached the inhabited Illinois village of Pimitoui [Peoria] on January 5, 1680, La Salle had an inspiration. They would build a new ship below Pimitoui, sail down the Mississippi, then cross the Gulf of Mexico to the French West Indies, or head round the Florida panhandle and follow the coast north to New France.

Six shipwrights deserted. Yet work went ahead on a forty-ton vessel that, like the *Griffon,* would serve as a floating fortress. And where was the *Griffon?* There had been no word of her since she had set sail for Niagara in mid-September. Had she been stolen, scuttled, wrecked or was she wintering at Niagara? La Salle could salvage sails, rigging and anchors for his new barque from the *Griffon,* if he could find her.

And where was the Mississippi? Louis Jolliet's accounts placed La Belle Rivière at the confluence of the Illinois, and in February, La Salle sent two men, with Father Hennepin, to reconnoitre. On March 1, leaving Tonty and a ragtag remnant of his expedition at a makeshift outpost, Fort Crèvecoeur, La Salle and five men set off in search of the *Griffon.* Paddling up ice-choked rivers, dragging their canoes through snowdrifts and slush, they reached Lake Michigan on March 24. When messengers from Michilimackinac confirmed that the *Griffon* was not on the lake, La Salle determined to reach Fort Niagara overland, on foot.

"We continued our march through the woods," La Salle writes, "which was so interlaced with thorns and brambles that our clothes were all torn and our faces so covered with blood that we hardly knew each other. On the 28th, we found the woods more open, and began to fare better, meeting a good deal of game, which after this rarely failed us; so that we no longer carried provisions with us, but made a meal of roast meat wherever we happened to kill a deer, bear, or turkey."

After wading for three days through a freezing marsh, harassed by Illinois hunters alarmed by the smoke from their fires, the party made an elm bark canoe and floated down a creek to Lake Erie. La Salle reached Fort Niagara on April 21. There was no trace of the *Griffon.* The men he had posted there eighteen months earlier paddled him down Lake Ontario and La Salle arrived at Fort Frontenac on May 6, 1680, completing an epic journey of nearly a thousand miles in sixty-five days.

And all for naught. Towards the end of July, as La Salle was organizing a new expedition, this time by canoe, to supply Fort Crèvecoeur and

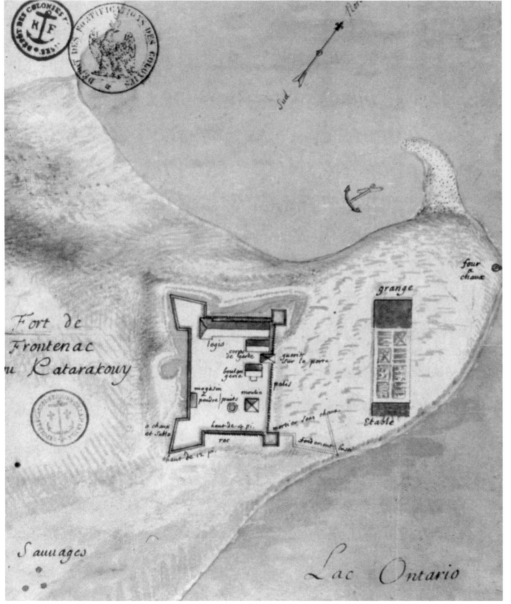

Fort de Frontenac u Cataraкouy

Lac Ontario

Sauuages

furnish his barque to explore the Mississippi, a letter came from Tonty saying that the men who had remained at Fort Crèvecoeur had mutinied, burned the fort, and thrown into the river everything they couldn't carry away. Hearing that the deserters were on Lake Ontario, on their way to kill him, La Salle recruited three canoes of loyal voyageurs and ambushed the fugitives at the Bay of Quinte; two were killed, and seven captured and jailed at Fort Frontenac.

Undaunted, La Salle departed again for the Illinois on August 10, 1680, with twenty-five men, including a surgeon, carpenters, masons, soldiers and a young lieutenant, Dauphin de la Forest. In a desperate hurry to find Henri Tonty and the Recollet fathers – nothing had been heard of Hennepin's expedition to the Mississippi – La Salle took a shortcut up the Toronto Carrying Place. In a letter he wrote a year later, he says: "I left Teioiagon on August 22nd and arrived on the shore of Lake Toronto [Simcoe] on the 23rd where I arrested two of my deserters, one named Gabriel Minime, and the other Grandmaison."

La Salle would take the northern route to Sault Ste. Marie and Michilimackinac, searching the rocky shores of Lake Huron for signs of Tonty or the lost *Griffon;* by Lake Erie, he sent "the Blacksmith, two seamen, two soldiers and a rope maker with iron, oakum, tar, sails and tools to finish the small craft along with three hundred pounds of lead, powder and guns with which to

reached a silent, blackened wasteland that had been the hospitable Illinois village, Pimitoui. Skeletons of the dead were strewn in the ashes of their lodges, their heads impaled on poles or branches. La Salle fearfully examined the skulls for a trace of Tonty's hair; Tonty's head was not among them. The massacre confirmed rumours that the Iroquois had gone to war against the Algonquian nations south of the Great Lakes, yet there were no signs that the Iroquois had occupied La Salle's fiefdom. Not a living soul was to be seen.

Camping overnight in this charnel house, La Salle writes: "I did not sleep a moment with trying to make up my mind as to what I ought to do." The prudent choice would be to retreat, but what if Tonty and the Recollet fathers, facing starvation, were waiting only a few leagues downriver at Fort Crèvecoeur?

Hiding three armed men on an island in charge of the baggage, La Salle set off downriver with four men in one canoe. The riverbanks were lined with abandoned campsites, Illinois on the west, Iroquois on the east; Iroquois chiefs had carved totems boasting the number of warriors they had commanded, but there were no signs of French prisoners. And there was no one in the ruins of Fort Crèvecoeur, only an ominous message scratched on the unfinished boat: *Nous sommes tous sauvages.*

Days later, La Salle reached the goal he had set himself more than ten years earlier:

Left: La Salle's Griffon *passes the flats of the St. Clair River.*

Opposite: Fort Frontenac at Cataraquin, 1685

arm ourselves … I had made them take this southern route because on the northern there is a spit of land one needs to cross through, thirteen leagues in width from Teioiagon to Lake Taronto, where one must transport all their baggage by the peak of very high mountains [the Oak Ridges Moraine] which, being heavily loaded, they would have had difficulties in doing and would have lost much time."

Still, it was December 1 before La Salle

the Mississippi River. Yet he resisted the temptation to launch his canoe into its strong, seductive current; it was winter, he was in enemy territory, and his soldiers, labourers, supplies and trade goods had been left behind on Lake Michigan. He fastened a letter for Tonty to a tree, and turned back. At the end of January 1681, having tramped for days through howling blizzards, La Salle and his companions reached safe haven at Fort St. Joseph, his post on Lake Michigan.

Cooped up in this isolated spot for the winter, La Salle had ample time to brood over his misfortunes, and blame everyone but himself. Refusing to admit that his visionary kingdom was impossible, if not insane, La Salle recreated himself as the champion of his massacred Algonquin allies against their common enemy, the Iroquois. "The tribes of the West might be taught to forget their mutual animosities, and join in a defensive league, with La Salle at its head," explains his biographer, Francis Parkman. "They might be colonized around his fort in the valley of the Illinois, where, in the shadow of the French flag, and with the aid of French allies, they could hold the Iroquois in check, and acquire in some measure the arts of a settled life. The Franciscan friars could teach them the Faith; and La Salle and his associates could supply them with goods, in exchange for the vast harvest of furs which their hunters could gather in these boundless wilds. Meanwhile, he would seek out the mouth of the Mississippi; and the

furs gathered at his colony in the Illinois would then find a ready passage to the markets of the world. Thus might this ancient slaughter-field of warring savages be redeemed to civilization and Christianity; and a stable settlement, half-feudal, half-commercial, grow up in the heart of the western wilderness."

As soon as the snow began to melt, La Salle made a circuit of Algonquin camps, many of them refugees from the Iroquois wars, exhorting them to live at peace with one another under the protection of the Great King. La Salle's courtly manners and florid oratory impressed the Miami and Illinois chiefs, and he won their allegiance with rich gifts: cloth, clothing, hunting knives, trinkets, brandy and guns. Before leaving for Québec in May, via Michilimackinac, where he found Tonty in good health, La Salle had recruited a private army of more than 100 warriors.

On his final expedition to the Mississippi across the Great Lakes, La Salle crossed the Toronto Carrying Place in late August 1681. It took two weeks to portage his canoes and baggage from Lake Ontario to Lake Simcoe, with La Salle grumbling about his Aboriginal porters: "I must speak to them continually, and bear all their importunity, or else they will do nothing I want."

A FEW DAYS before Christmas, the expedition, twenty-five Frenchmen, including Tonty and Recollet priest Zenobe Membré, and eighteen

La Salle's Expedition to Louisiana in 1684, by Theodore Gudon. The painting is set in Matagorda Bay. The ship on the left is the La Belle, *the remains of which were recently discovered. The* Le Joly *dominates the centre of the painting while the* L'Aimable, *at the rear, has run aground.*

natives with ten wives and three children, struck off up the frozen rivers south of Lake Michigan, dragging their canoes and provisions on sledges until they reached open water south of Lake Peoria. There were no Iroquois, and the villages they passed were empty. On February 6, 1682, they reached the Mississippi at the mouth of the Illinois, and floated downstream past the confluences of the Missouri and Ohio rivers until, on March 13, they reached the Arkansas, not far from where Jolliet and Marquette had turned back in 1673. When La Salle displayed the calumet, or peace pipe, to the apprehensive Quapaws, they welcomed these strangers with feasts, dancing and caresses, and guided them south into a marshy country of alligators and villages of exotic, but friendly, sun-worshippers.

On April 6, 1682, the expedition entered a vast delta where the Mississippi divided into three channels. The water tasted of salt, the air smelled of the sea and René-Robert Cavelier de La Salle gazed at last on the Gulf of Mexico. Three days later, assembling his men on a high point of land upriver, he planted a column and

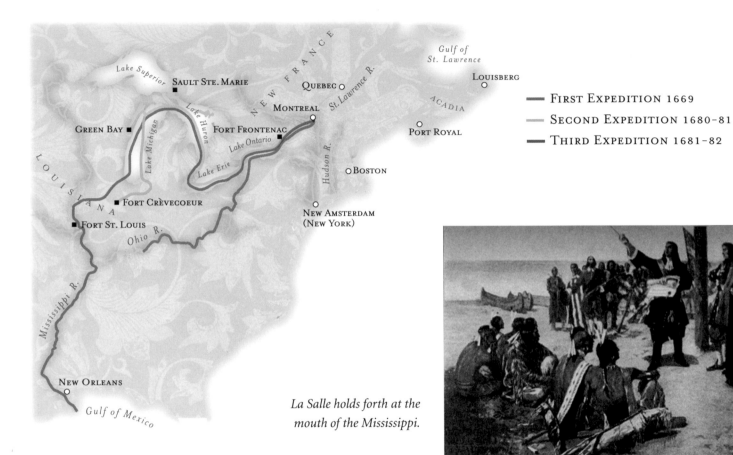

Map labels:

Gulf of St. Lawrence

Lake Superior · SAULT STE. MARIE · N E W   F R A N C E · QUEBEC · LOUISBERG

Lake Huron · MONTREAL · St. Lawrence R. · ACADIA

GREEN BAY · Lake Michigan · FORT FRONTENAC · PORT ROYAL

Lake Ontario · Lake Erie · Hudson R.

L O U I S I A N A · FORT CRÈVECOEUR · ○ BOSTON

FORT ST. LOUIS · Ohio R. · NEW AMSTERDAM (NEW YORK)

Mississippi R.

NEW ORLEANS

Gulf of Mexico

— FIRST EXPEDITION 1669
— SECOND EXPEDITION 1680–81
— THIRD EXPEDITION 1681–82

La Salle holds forth at the mouth of the Mississippi.

buried a lead plate bearing the arms of France. Following Father Membré's blessings, volleys of gunfire and shouts of *Vive le Roi!* La Salle proclaimed: "In the name of the most high, mighty, invincible, and victorious Prince, Louis the Great, by the Grace of God King of France and Navarre, Fourteenth of that name, I, this ninth day of April, one thousand six hundred and eighty-two, in virtue of the commission of his Majesty, which I hold in my hand, and which may be seen by all whom it may concern, have taken, and do now take, in the name of his Majesty and of his successors to the crown, possession of this country of Louisiana, the seas, harbours, ports, bays, adjacent straits, and all the nations, peoples, provinces, cities, towns, villages, mines, minerals, fisheries, streams and rivers, within the extent of said Louisiana ..."

More than a year passed before La Salle returned to Québec to report his triumph in person, and to find that he was ruined. His five-year monopoly on trade in the western Mississippi had expired, and the king, preoccupied with his European wars, mistresses and entertainments, had decided "the discovery of the Sieur de la Salle is very useless." New France's new governor, Le Febvre de la Barre, had come to believe that La Salle had lied about his discovery, and "instead of returning to the colony to learn what the king wishes him to do, he does not come near me, but keeps in the backwoods, five hundred leagues off, with the idea of attracting the inhabitants to him, and building up an imaginary kingdom for himself, by debauching all the bankrupts and idlers of this country."

La Salle had sent to the governor no maps or log books of his Mississippi journey, or reliable witnesses, and in December 1682, in defiance of warnings of Iroquois attacks, he had built Fort St. Louis on a steep cliff overlooking the Illinois River. Silhouetted against the sky, the palisaded fort acted as a beacon to La Salle's frightened Algonquin allies; thousands camped around it, expecting the protection of the Great King. But La Salle, with only Henri Tonty and twenty Frenchmen, had little ammunition and nothing to feed his new colonists. La Salle's messengers, sent to Québec with orders for munitions and supplies, were arrested as illegal traders; La Barre, convinced that La Salle was inciting a war with the Iroquois that threatened to destroy New France, ignored his frantic letters. He seized his seigneury, Fort Frontenac, and as La Salle sailed for France, sent troops to occupy Fort St. Louis.

La Salle never returned to Canada. Instead, he sailed to the Gulf of Mexico with a convoy of ships carrying settlers to found a colony at the mouth of the Mississippi River. On March 19, 1687, he was murdered by his own Frenchmen, an act of revenge for a chimerical colonization scheme destroyed in a malarial swamp by fever and starvation. La Salle's debts, owed largely to his family, amounted to almost 500,000 livres.

La Salle has no grave; his corpse was tossed into the bushes to be devoured by animals. A privileged son of a despotic, corrupt, feudal society, he had all the vices, and virtues, of his class, united with a peasant's physical strength, the charm of a courtesan, and a mystical talent for destruction. His heirs on the Great Lakes were the Canadian *coureurs de bois* who, unlike the king, eagerly occupied the empire La Salle had claimed for himself.

Seventeenth-century travellers and traders faced a host of challenges, not least of which were the Great Lakes themselves.

Turbulent Times

In the turbulent final decades of the seventeenth century, with France at war with the Iroquois in North America, and with England in Europe, hundreds of independent free traders, French, English and Dutch, pedalled their wares throughout the Great Lakes as far west as the Missouri River and Lake of the Woods.

Located on a side road on the Oak Ridges Moraine near King City, this sign is an indication of the region's growing interest in its fascinating history.

BARRY WALLACE

ALL BUT the few who were licensed by the governor of New France did so illegally, secretly supplied with trade goods by wealthy speculators, including the colonial administrators who had outlawed them, and, it was whispered, the Jesuits. Though the traders' annual harvest of furs was the mainstay of New France's economy, these "wild men of the forest", vilified as renegades, thieves, drunkards and fornicators, were liable to be arrested, or murdered, by military patrols and aggrieved creditors. The wooded valleys and meandering streams of the Toronto Carrying Place, and the dark swamps of the Nottawasaga River's eastern tributaries, afforded them a safer passage to the Northwest than the heavily travelled route via the Ottawa River; Iroquois ambushes made the south shore of Lake Ontario impassable to any Frenchman, trader or soldier.

By the end of the century, no Iroquois remained on the north shore. In 1687, some 400 Odawa, Ojibwe and Mississauga warriors had travelled south from Lake Huron to join a French attack on the Iroquois homeland; they either wiped out Teiaiagon and the other Iroquois river villages, or the Iroquois, fighting a guerrilla war of attrition to the south and east, had already abandoned them.

By the time France and England declared peace in 1698, and the Iroquois, decimated by war and disease, agreed to remain south of the Great Lakes, the Mississauga were occupying the

Toronto Carrying Place, the mouth of the river, and the north shores of Lake Ontario and Lake Erie. They called the Humber River Cobechenonk – "leave the canoes and go back".

A plain-living, traditional people, for nearly a century the Mississauga would enjoy relative quiet and prosperity far from the warfare and rebellions that raged around them. In Europe, the market for fur was glutted, and the fur-bearing animals around the Great Lakes had been trapped almost to extinction. It was 1720 before the French ventured to build a tiny government trading post, *un magasin royal*, overlooking the river on the bluff once occupied by Teiaiagon. Managed by three Montréal brothers, Jean, Alexandre and Philippe Douville, with two soldiers and one merchant, it closed ten years later, unable to compete with its French rival, Fort Niagara, or with a new English fort, Oswego, on Lake Ontario's south shore. The Mississauga willingly paddled the extra miles for better quality English goods at cheaper prices.

At last, in the summer of 1749, a French officer, Portneuf, set up shop at the mouth of the river with competitive merchandise and laid the groundwork for a permanent post on a flat, rocky outcrop overlooking the lake about two miles to the east. Five timber buildings, set in a square 180 feet to a side and surrounded by a palisade, Fort Rouillé – named for French Colonial Minister Antoine Rouillé – housed seven soldiers, one officer, a storekeeper and labourers. Everyone called it Fort Toronto, and it was the future City

LIZ SAUL

Yesterday and tomorrow: An obelisk marks the spot where Fort Rouillé once stood, while behind it, a wind turbine provides energy for the future.

Trading at Fort Rouillé, as depicted by
Frederick S. Challener in 1928

of Toronto's first permanent building.

"The wine here is of the best," noted François Piquet, a Sulpician priest who visited in June 1752. "Nothing is wanting in the fort; everything is abundant, fine and good."

Good French brandy likely explained Fort Toronto's popularity with the Mississauga; it may have been better than the English rum at Oswego. Officially forbidden to trade brandy, the French offered it as a gift. It was a powerful attraction, and when a crowd of agitated Mississauga warriors suddenly surrounded Fort Toronto in the summer of 1757, the nervous commander jumped to the conclusion that they had come to pillage his kegs of brandy. He sent two men in a canoe to Fort Niagara to summon reinforcements, and the next day six French soldiers in two bateaux with swivel guns mounted in their bows rowed past the fort firing volleys of musket balls into the air. A parley with the astonished Mississauga revealed that the warriors were going to Montréal to help their French allies fend off an English invasion.

Two years later, to avoid its capture by the English, the French evacuated Fort Toronto and burned it to the ground.

British soldiers captured Fort Niagara in the summer of 1759; Québec fell in September, Montréal a year later. But the victorious British troops were so slow to occupy the French posts on the western Great Lakes that they were beaten to Michilimackinac by a daredevil twenty-two-

LIBRARY AND ARCHIVES CANADA / C-014253

year-old New Jersey trader, Alexander Henry. Purchasing English goods in Albany, New York, Henry left Montreal on August 3, 1761, amid alarming rumours that an Odawa war chief, Pontiac, was threatening to seize Detroit and toss the English back into the sea. As a precaution, Henry placed his canoe brigade in charge of a French Canadian manager, Étienne Campion, and his veteran voyageurs; Campion and his men were among the first Quebeçois to switch their allegiance to *les Anglais,* but they were not alone. Crossing Lake Huron, Henry was so frightened by Ojibwe warnings that Pontiac's warriors would kill the first Englishman they met, he disguised himself: "I laid aside my English clothes, and covered myself only with a cloth, passed about the middle; a shirt, hanging loose; a

Though it would make history as the first permanent building in the City of Toronto, Fort Rouillé was a simple construction, as shown here in 1750.

molton, or blanket coat; and a large, red, milled worsted cap. The next thing was to smear my face and hands with dirt and grease; and this done, I took the place of one of my men."

Henry's childish ruse, instantly discovered by the Ojibwe at Michilimackinac, made everyone laugh, and his gift to the Ojibwe chief of "English milk", a small keg of rum, won their friendship. The proud, fractious, Algonquin nations were agonizing over an impossible dilemma; should they join Pontiac's resistance or, by using diplomacy, turn the English invasion to their own advantage? This Englishman's canoes, loaded with tons of hatchets, knives, cloth, kettles and rum destined for the Northwest, argued persuasively in favour of an alliance. Characteristically, it was expressed as a dream: "Wa'Wa'Tam began to come often to my house," Henry writes in his memoir, *Travels and Adventures in Canada and the Indian Territories*, "betraying, in his demeanour, strong marks of personal regard.

After this had continued for some time, he came on a certain day, bringing with him his whole family, and, at the same time, a large present consisting of skins, sugar, and dried meat. Having laid these in a heap, he commenced a speech, in which he informed me that some years before he had observed a fast, devoting himself, according to the custom of his nation, to solitude, and to the mortification of his body, in the hope to obtain, from the Great Spirit, protection through all his days; that on this occasion

PHOTOS: PETER ST. JOHN

being "made into a broth". At Michilimackinac in May 1763, Henry was astonished when Wa'Wa'Tam and his wife arrived, warning him of "the noise of evil birds"; Pontiac's warriors, furious that the peace treaty between Britain and France excluded the Algonquin empire, were intending to massacre all of the English intruders. Henry had noticed that hundreds of Odawa and Ojibwe were camped around the post, but it was trading season, and he was pleased by their keen interest in his tomahawks and silver bracelets. Major George Etherington, commander of Michilimackinac's garrison of ninety soldiers, scoffed at the rumours, and Henry rejected Wa'Wa'Tam's tearful offer to join his family at their summer camp.

On June 4, 1763, the King's birthday, the Odawa and Ojibwe invited the entire garrison to a festive game of lacrosse on a field outside the palisade. Henry stayed in his room, writing letters. Distracted by the game's shrieks and whoops, he looked out his window; the natives had invaded the garrison, and were clubbing, scalping and disemboweling every soldier they could grab. Henry took refuge with his neighbour, the former French commander, Mouet de Langlade, but the next day de Langlade turned him over to a crowd of intoxicated chiefs who were fighting among themselves; should they hold their prisoners for ransom, or kill them on the spot? Stripped naked, with only a blanket around his shoulders, Henry was dumped into a canoe and, with other captured English traders,

he had dreamed of adopting an Englishman, as his son, brother and friend; that from the moment in which he first beheld me, he had recognized me as the person whom the Great Spirit had been pleased to point out to him for a brother; that he hoped that I would not refuse his present; and that he should forever regard me as one of his family.

Wa'Wa'Tam and Henry went their separate ways; Henry spent most of the next year in Sault Ste. Marie establishing an alliance with a Canadian trader and interpreter, Jean-Baptiste Cadotte, and his Ojibwe wife, Athanasie. Waiting for his canoes to return from the Northwest, Henry travelled freely, hearing no Ojibwe threats of

Built around 1715, on the south shore of the Straits of Mackinac, which link Lake Huron and Lake Michigan, Fort Michilimackinac, left, was first a French, and later British trading post. Today the fort is a U.S. National Historic Landmark, located in Mackinaw City, Michigan.

Just across the strait is Mackinac Island, where the British rebuilt Fort Michilimackinac following the fall of its namesake on the mainland. Today it is known as Fort Mackinac.

paddled from camp to camp to learn his fate.

On June 7, a welcome figure loomed out of the smoky gloom of an Ojibwe wigwam. "He is my brother," said Wa'Wa'Tam, and led Henry away to a new life as an Ojibwe:

My hair was cut off, and my head shaved, with the exception of a spot on the crown. My face was painted with three or four different colours; some parts of it red, others black. A shirt was provided for me, painted with vermillion, mixed with grease. A large collar of wampum was put round my neck, and another suspended on my breast. Both my arms were decorated with large bands of silver above the elbow, besides several smaller ones on the wrists; and my legs were covered with mi-tasses, a kind of hose, made as is the favourite fash-ion, of scarlet cloth. Over all, I was to wear a scarlet blanket or mantle, and on my head a large bunch of feathers. I parted, not without some regret, with the long hair which was natural to it, and which I fancied to be ornamental, but the ladies of the family, and of the village in general, appeared to think my person improved, and now condescended to call me handsome, even among Indians.

FOR THE next year, Henry lived in disguise in Wa'Wa'Tam's village. Apart from the lack of con-versation, even though he spoke Ojibwe well, he enjoyed the fishing, hunting and trapping and accumulated his own stock of beaver to trade. He had no choice; all of his goods, including his

canoes, had been pillaged by his enemies during the Michilimackinac massacre. Seventy soldiers and one officer had been murdered.

But Henry's luck held. Spying a canoe with a white sail against the horizon, he learned that Sir William Johnson, Indian Commissioner, had sent an invitation to the Ojibwe of Sault Ste. Marie to negotiate a peace treaty at Fort Niagara. Fort Niagara was the first step on Henry's return to Montreal, and from there he would have the protection of the King of England. Once again disguised as a voyageur, Henry attached himself to the Ojibwe delegation. They travelled across Lake Huron and up the Severn River.

On the 18th of June [1764], we crossed Lake aux Claies [Simcoe], which appeared to be upward of twenty miles in length. At its further end we came to the carrying-place of Toranto. Here the Indians obliged me to carry a burden of more than a hundred pounds weight. The day was very hot, and the woods and marshes abounded with mosquitoes; but the Indians walked at a quick pace, and I could by no means see myself left behind. The whole country was a thick forest, through which our only road was a foot-path, or such as, in America, is exclu-sively termed an 'Indian path'.

The next morning, at ten o'clock, we reached the shore of Lake Ontario. Here we employed two days in making canoes out of the bark of the elm-tree, in which we were to transport ourselves to Niagara.

Reaching Fort Niagara in the morning, the Ojibwe delegation, sixteen of the most powerful chiefs and elders in the Northwest, was greeted warmly by Sir William Johnson. But there were no treaty negotiations; the Ojibwe diplomats, together with eighty from Lake aux Claies, were summarily conscripted into an "Indian Battalion", commanded by Alexander Henry, to accompany General John Bradstreet and 3,000 British troops to raise Pontiac's siege of Fort Detroit.

"The next day," Henry writes, without surprise, "I found that they had all deserted, going back to their homes, equipments and all, by the way of Toronto."

They were, after all, at peace with their kinsmen at Detroit, and prepared to live in peace with the British; British troops would be welcomed back to Michilimackinac, and the Ojibwe, having held their commanding officer, Major Etherington, for ransom, would not be punished for the slaughter of his garrison. Henry may have owed his freedom, and his life, to one of the leaders of this delegation, the Toronto Mississauga chief Wabbicommicot. Having pledged loyalty to the British after the Conquest, Wabbicommicot became good friends with Sir William Johnson, who treated him as the "Chief Man North & West upon Lake Ontario", and had kept the warriors under his influence out of the conflict. Wabbicommicot himself adopted the role of conciliator, and now went to Fort Detroit to attempt to negotiate a peaceful end to the long

siege at an assembly of more than two thousand Algonquin chiefs and warriors. Like the Ojibwe who had sheltered Henry at Michilmackinac, Wabbicommicot understood that they were dependent on the British for guns, ammunition, ironware, blankets and clothing that the French had supplied, and that the Algonquin nations' military power – they had seized eight forts – had put the British on the defensive. All the British require, protested Sir William, "is to live at peace with you & carry on Trade".

As the British redcoats hurried off to the west,

The Seige of Fort Detroit in 1763, *as depicted by Frederic Remington*

The wetlands of Minesing Swamp are protected and valued today, much as they were by the Mississauga.

with Alexander Henry in hot pursuit of his stolen trade goods, and the new colonial administration at Quebec puzzled over what to do with half of North America, the north shore of Lake Ontario entered a brief twilight of tranquility before the next invasion. The pines whispered in the breezes, rapids muttered to themselves; nesting waterfowl choked the marshes, and colonies of beaver and muskrat once again flourished in the Nottawasaga swamps. The Mississauga people lived much as their ancestors had thousands of years before. Fishnets, hooks and harpoons were simple to make, deer and small game could be snared or trapped, a treed bear brought down with spears or a hail of stones. Medicinal plants, plums, grapes and berries of all kinds were there for the picking, the spring salmon run an occasion for feasting. In the hot, humid summer months, they camped

LIZ SAUL

WALKING INTO WILDERNESS: THE TORONTO CARRYING PLACE AND NINE MILE PORTAGE

on islands in the inland lakes, or on the sandspit curving into Lake Ontario east of the Toronto River. From here, on a clear day, they could see the mist from Niagara Falls, and traders came from Fort Niagara to barter rum, their irresistible, deadly European import.

In the spring of 1770, a strange canoe, paddled by Canadians, came from the east. It turned up the Toronto River and landed not far below the overgrown ruins of Teiaiagon. The passenger, dressed in the English fashion, sat amid bales of merchandise and kegs of rum. Jean Bonaventure Rousseaux, recently appointed an interpreter with the Indian Department, spoke the Mississauga language fluently. He had come not so much as a trader, but as an emissary from King George III with gifts for His Majesty's new subjects.

Rousseaux, from Montreal, had not hesitated to swear allegiance to the British crown. He may have had no choice, since the overwhelming majority of New France's great merchants and landowners, the bourgeois who financed the fur trade, eagerly accepted pensions, commissions and offices in the administration of Governor Sir Guy Carleton. Faced with governing a conquered people, including 7,500 native North Americans, with 1,500 British troops, Carleton pursued a policy of cooperation and conciliation; he strengthened the stable, authoritarian social structures of the *ancien régime,* including recognition of French language and civil law, and of Roman Catholicism as the Established Church. Carleton,

an Irish aristocrat and career soldier, saw the future with unusual clarity: "Barring a catastrophe shocking to think of, this country must, to the end of time, be peopled by the Canadian race."

European loyalties no longer mattered. In the 200 and more years since the first Europeans had jumped ship, thousands more had informally immigrated, establishing, over generations, a population that was neither European nor Aboriginal but truly indigenous. Canadians identified themselves with their extended families, and with a place, a parish perhaps, or a landmark: the Ojibwe of Sault Ste. Marie were known as the Saulteurs.

To inspire Canadians with "a cordial attachment and zeal for the King's Government", Carleton encouraged agriculture and village industries, and promoted the expansion of the fur trade to the Mississippi and the Northwest. The Canadians could do as they pleased, as long as they had a British trading partner, and these swarmed into Montreal like bees to a hive. In this invigorating new economy, a Canadian like Jean Bonaventure Rousseaux, able to read, write and count well enough to keep a good ledger – no easy task when he was trading sturgeon oil for white muslin – could become a rich man.

When Jean Bonaventure died in 1774, at the outbreak of the American Revolution, his seventeen-year-old son, Jean-Baptiste Rousseaux, inherited his father's position as trader and interpreter with the Indian Department with an annual salary of two pairs of strong moccasins and 300

The certificate of the 1795 marriage between Jean-Baptiste Rousseaux and Margaret Clyne

British pounds sterling. During the long, bloody course of the Revolutionary War, Jean-Baptiste's role seems to have been to keep the Algonquin north of Lake Ontario loyal to the British Crown, and to act as a liaison with the Loyalist Iroquois war chief, Joseph Brant, whose warriors were harassing the American army in New York state. When the Iroquois were resettled on two million acres of land along the Grand River north of Lake Erie – the best land in Canada – after the British surrender, they became Rousseaux's best customers. Brant actively solicited Canadian investors like Rousseaux and his British partners to build mills, smithies and stores in his vast new wilderness homeland. In 1787, Rousseaux married Brant's adoptive daughter, Margaret Clyne, reputedly the orphaned child of British settlers killed by the Iroquois, and soon after built a homestead for his family at the Carrying Place on the east bank of the Toronto River. A substantial building forty feet square, it would have included a storehouse and trading room, and possibly a stable for a cow. It was the City of Toronto's first home.

The Rousseaux family was not alone; by 1788 gangs of surveyors, harassed by angry Mississauga, were tramping through the woods with clanking chains, and wading waist-deep through marshes, measuring the landscape into neat squares and rectangles for a prospective townsite with a hinterland of farms. Thousands of British Loyalists, persecuted by the triumphant Americans, or enticed by Britain's offer of 200 acres of free land

and provisions for one year, were clamouring to resettle north of Lake Ontario. Land grants, awarded by Governor Carleton, now Lord Dorchester, and his advisors in Quebec, were based on patronage, speculation and pleading letters. Rousseaux, who had no legal title to his homestead, faced two powerful rivals for control of the Toronto Carrying Place. The North West Company of Montreal had for years petitioned for a land grant permitting them to carry their canoe brigades and fur trade merchandize over the portage from Lake Ontario to Lake Huron, but Dorchester preferred a more grandiose proposal put forward by an importunate French-Canadian army officer, Philippe François de Rastel, Sieur de Rocheblave.

During the American Revolution, Rocheblave had commanded Kaskaskia, an old French trading post and Jesuit mission on the Mississippi, renamed Fort Gage, because the native people hated the English. In 1778, the Americans took the fort without a fight, capturing Rocheblave asleep in his bed; two years later, he escaped from a Virginia prison and made his way back to Quebec.

As compensation for his suffering and loss of property, Rocheblave requested a grant of 1,000 acres on Toronto Bay – roughly from the ruins of Fort Rouillé to the Rouge River, as well as additional grants for his wife, four children, and a dozen hangers-on. Moreover, Rocheblave wanted a monopoly on all transport over the Toronto Carrying Place between Lake Ontario and Lake La Claie, provided that the government built him a wagon road, and indemnified him against "all carriages, horses and oxen taken away or destroyed by the Indians".

Rocheblave received his 1,000 acres, with no transportation monopoly, in 1791, but the grant was immediately nullified by the creation of the new province of Upper Canada; Lieutenant-Governor John Graves Simcoe had his own plans for the western frontier of British North America.

The armorial bearings of the North West Company

With calm, sky-blue water, Lake Simcoe sometimes seems a place apart. In fact, known by many names and travelled by many peoples, it has been at the heart of Southern Ontario history for millennia.

John Graves Simcoe:

A Brief Tenure and Lasting Mark

John Graves Simcoe,

with his elfin wife Elizabeth

and their two youngest children,

arrived at the new province's provisional capital,

Newark, a swampy, decrepit outpost of Fort Niagara,

in June 1792.

*John Graves Simcoe,
as painted by Jean
Laurent Mosnier*

H IS FIRST, urgent task was to move the capital to a new location secure from American attack. In the peace treaty of 1783, Britain had surrendered its historic claim to all territory south of the Great Lakes, including its forts at Niagara, Detroit and Michilimackinac. But the treaty had not yet been ratified by the United States Senate, and the concession of the Ohio and eastern Mississippi Valleys so enraged the British public, and Britain's betrayed Algonquin allies, that Britain found excuses not to evacuate the forts. If Fort Niagara did pass into American hands, Newark would be at the mercy of its guns.

Toronto, known to the colonial administration from surveyors' reports and the agitations of Rocheblave and the North West Company, was the favoured site. In May 1793, Simcoe and a group of officers cruised Lake Ontario's western shore inspecting potential harbours; Toronto Bay, sheltered by a low, wooded sandspit crooked like a beckoning finger, impressed Simcoe with its strategic potential. The water was clear and translucent, but was it deep enough for naval vessels? A Canadian sailor, Joseph Bouchette, was assigned to the survey. Bouchette wrote later:

I still distinctly recollect the untamed aspect which the country exhibited when first I entered the beautiful basin, which thus became the scene of my early hydrographical operations. Dense and trackless forests lined the margin of the lake and reflected

110

their inverted images in its glassy surface …
beneath their luxuriant foliage [was a] group then
consisting of two families of Mississagas [sic], …
[T]he bay and the neighbouring marshes were the
hitherto uninvaded haunts of immense coveys of
wild fowel [sic]. Indeed they were so abundant as
in some measure to annoy us during the night.

Simcoe garrisoned Toronto without delay; his only troops were two companies of Queen's Rangers, remnants of a Loyalist reconnaissance corps he had commanded during the Revolutionary War, armed with a few old cannon. By the end of July, the Rangers were camped on the rocky shoreline of Toronto Bay east of old Fort Rouillé, and land had been cleared for the Simcoes' canvas house, a spacious, airy tent Simcoe had purchased from the estate of the famed explorer, Captain James Cook.

On Monday, July 29, Elizabeth Simcoe wrote in her diary:

We were prepared to sail for Toronto this morning,
but the wind changed suddenly. We dined with the
Chief Justice, and were recalled from a walk at nine
o'clock this evening, as the wind had become fair.
We embarked on board the Mississaga, the band
playing in the ship. It was dark, and so I went to
bed and slept until eight o'clock the next morning
when I found myself in the harbour of Toronto.
We had gone under an easy sail all night, for as
no person on board had ever been at Toronto,

This portrait of Elizabeth Simcoe, dressed in traditional Welsh costume to reflect her ancestry, was painted by Mary Ann Burgess in 1790.

LIBRARY AND ARCHIVES CANADA, ACC. NO. 1972-118-2 / C-095815

Mr. Bouchette was afraid to enter the harbour till daylight, when St. John Rousseau, an Indian trader who lives near, came on board to pilot us.

Jean-Baptiste Rousseaux, or Mr. St. John, as the Simcoes liked to call him, to the point of calling the Toronto River where he lived "St. John's Creek", became indispensable as a guide, mediator and host. By August 1793, Simcoe was inspecting a mill on St. John's Creek a short distance above Rousseaux's homestead. "The Gov. brought me some very good Cakes," Elizabeth

Scottish born, Alexander Macdonell, right, was living in New York State before coming to Canada in 1781 as a member of Butler's Rangers. He served as sheriff for the Home District of York between 1792 and 1805. A year earlier in 1804, he was elected to the Parliament of Upper Canada and served as speaker until 1808.

writes in her diary on August 6. "The Miller's Wife is from the United States where the women excel in making Cakes & bread."

The Carrying Place was also one of the few clear trails where she could ride on horseback: "4th of September," she writes, "I rode to St. John's Creek. There is a ridge of land extending near a mile, beyond St. John's House, 300 feet high & not more than three feet wide, the bank towards the river is of smooth turf. There is a great deal of Hemlock Spruce on this river, the banks are dry & pleasant. I gathered a beautiful species of Polygala."

Caesar of his wilderness, Simcoe envisioned a chain of military posts to protect western Upper Canada from American invasion. He began by anglicizing the landscape: Toronto was renamed York, in honour of the king's son, the Duke of York; the site for a possible new capital on the La Tranche River was named London, and the river's name changed to the Thames. York's central river became the Don, St. John's Creek, the Humber River. A road to be named Dundas was surveyed all the way to London, and in September 1793, Simcoe led a military reconnaissance expedition up the Toronto Carrying Place to Lake La Claie and Matchetache Bay on Lake Huron.

TORONTO PUBLIC LIBRARY, JOHN ROSS ROBERTSON COLLECTION

He was accompanied by his constant companion, a New-foundland dog named Jack Snap, along with Lieutenant Pilkington of the Royal Engineers, Lieutenant Darling of the 5th Regiment, Lieutenant Givens of the Queen's Rangers, surveyor Alexander Aitken, a dozen soldiers, four Ojibwe guides and Alexander Macdonell, sheriff of the Home District, who kept a diary of the journey:

1793, September 24th. Embarked in a batteau and went that night to Mr. St. John's on the Humber.

25th. Got up at daybreak to prepare matters for our journey. His Excellency Lieutenant-General Simcoe joined us from York. We shortly afterwards were ready and entered the woods, keeping our course N.N.W., crossed a long pine ridge. About one o'clock, dined upon a small river which empties itself into the Humber, and, to make the loads lighter, took the bones out of the pork. After dinner, re-loaded our horses and pursued our journey. About four o'clock, it beginning to rain, we encamped on the side of the Humber at the west extremity of the 3rd concession. We here got some wild grapes and a quantity of cray-fish.

26th. At eight o'clock continued our journey. In the early part of the day went over a pine ridge; but from ten till six in the evening, when we encamped, went through excellent land for grain or grass, the trees uncommonly large and tall, especially the pine. Crossed two small creeks which emptied themselves into the Humber, on one of which [Drunken Creek] we dined, and encamped on the second. The land through which we passed is chiefly wooded with maple, bass, beech, pine and cedar. During this day's march we passed the encampment of an Indian trader, who was on his way to his wintering ground on Lake La Claie.

27th. Proceeded on early in the morning. Shortly after leaving our fires went through a ridge of very fine pine, which appeared to be bounded by a deep ravine on the north. After crossing in an oblique direction the pine ridge, went over excellent land, black rich mould; timber, maple, beech, black birch and bass. Crossed a ravine and ascended a small eminence of indifferent land. This height terminated in a point, and a gradual descent to the River Humber, which we crossed. We dined here, and remained two hours to refresh ourselves and horses … After dinner proceeded on. Went over very uneven ground, the soil in some places indifferent, but in general not bad land. About six o'clock came to the end of the carrying place and encamped. Here we found Mr. Cuthbertson, Indian trader, and owner of the hut we passed the day before, encamped.

The swampy campsite, on the north side of the Oak Ridges Moraine, bordered Micicaguean Creek. Here, the Ojibwe had cached five canoes to take the expedition to Lake La Claie and Georgian Bay. On September 28, the soldiers built a crude bridge and a dock to load their provisions, and the expedition embarked about 4 p.m. Writes Macdonell:

We dragged our canoes till we came to the river, over a part of the swamp where it would be impossible to walk without their support, it being a quagmire, the skin or surface of which was very thin. Proceeded about a mile and a half or two miles along the river, which in this short distance has several turns. Went about a quarter of a mile up a smaller river which empties itself into the former and encamped. Soon after making our fires, the Great Sail and his family (Messessagues), who were encamped further up the river, came to visit their Great Father, the Lieutenant Governor, to whom they presented a pair of ducks, some beaver's meat, and a beaver's tail. His Excellency gave them some rum and tobacco.

29th. Embarked into our canoes in the same manner as the preceding day, paddled down the river, which is dead water, bordered on each side with quagmires, similar to the one we had hauled our canoes over … At twenty minutes after one we entered Lake La Claie, now Lake Simcoe, so called in memory of Captain Simcoe of the R.N.

GOVERNOR SIMCOE'S father, John, had died on board his ship in the Gulf of St. Lawrence prior to the British capture of Quebec in 1759. His only son, seven-year-old John Graves, became the responsibility of his godfather, Admiral Samuel Graves, a guardian he shared with his future wife, orphaned Elizabeth Gwillim. Captain James Cook had sailed under Captain Simcoe before achieving fame as an explorer, so Lake Simcoe's southern bay became Cook or Cook's Bay, the two neighbouring townships, East and West Gwillimbury. Simcoe must have been feeling less sentimental when he renamed the stagnant quagmire the Holland River for Canada's Dutch-born surveyor-general, Samuel Johannes Holland.

"At the entrance of the Lake," Macdonell continues, "we saw two canoes, who upon seeing us paddled off to their village, which was upon a point about four miles off, to apprise them of the Governor's arrival.

We paddled on towards the point and passed the village close in shore. The Indians, who were by this time assembled, fired a feu de joie *to compliment His Excellency, which we answered with three cheers, and then doubled the point, and put in shore in a small sandy bay to dine.*

Soon after our landing the Indians came in a body to wait on the Governor, to whom they presented a beaver blanket, which he declined taking then, but promised to take it on his return from Matchetache Bay. His Excellency was sorry that he could not see Keenees [or Canise], the chief of the village, with whom he was acquainted, as he was dangerously ill … After dinner we re-embarked, and the wind being fair, hoisted sail, and about dark put in shore and encamped in a cedar grove about six miles from the village.

The next day, as the five canoes sailed north past the deep, western bay leading to the Nottawasaga River portage to Lake Huron, Simcoe named it for another of his father's military colleagues, Robert Kempenfelt. On October 1, they reached the narrows where, in 1615, Champlain and Brûlé had departed south with their Huron war party, and entered the Matchetache [Severn] River. Four days later, after seven scenic but difficult portages around waterfalls and rapids, they arrived at George Cowan's trading post on Matchetache Bay. Suspecting the depth of water was too shallow for naval vessels, Simcoe paid a brief visit, in high winds, to the mouth of nearby Penetanguishene Harbour before heading home on October 6. On October 10, they camped once again

Opposite: A photograph of DeGrassi Point, taken in 1912 by Albert Hunter. Keenees's village was located on the point.

at Keenees's village, saddened to find that the chief had been dead for some days. About six o'clock, a number of women came to visit the governor. Macdonell writes:

Two of them carried the images of their deceased husbands, dolls about two feet long, decorated with silver broaches, feathers, paint, etc., if a chief, as was the case with one of these [Keenees], his medal is hung to his neck, the face painted black. His Excellency gave them some knives and look-ing-glasses, and shortly after they retired. At 8 o'clock the Indians came back in a body, and being seated around the fire, each got a dram and a piece of tobacco, after which the chief got up, thanked their Great Father, and presented him with the beaver blanket, which he spread under him. He then said: 'You white men pray; we poor Indians do not know what it is, but we hope you will entreat the Great Spirit to remove the sickness from amongst us.' To which the Gov-ernor replied that they should certainly be re-membered in the prayers of the whites. He then ordered them a keg of rum, and they went away perfectly happy, and highly pleased that the blan-ket was accepted, and that they had made their Father's bed.

Simcoe planned to walk to York by a differ-ent overland route, an old native trail that ran from what Macdonell calls "the landing place at the red pine fort", on an eastern branch of the Holland River, across the height of land to the headwaters of the Don and Rouge Rivers. How-ever, one of the Rangers, John Vincall, having nearly severed his toe in an accident, could not walk. On October 11, Simcoe ordered Macdonell, with Givens and a servant, McEwen, to return with Vincall to their old camp at the end of the Toronto Carrying Place, promising that he would send a horse for Vincall as soon as he arrived in York.

They arrived at the campsite at sunset on October 12 with almost nothing to eat; Macdonell shot a bittern for their dinner.

13th. Mr. Givens and his servant went out very early in the morning to hunt ducks. Vincall and I remained behind to pound and boil Indian corn for our breakfast. They returned about two o'clock with two ducks only. About half an hour before sunset Mr. Givens and I went up the river to get some birch bark to make torches to spear fish. On our way up fired repeatedly at ducks without any success; killed one but could not find it.

The following day, with only two quarts of corn and a small piece of pork remaining, Mac-donell and Givens resolved to seek help from the village. On the way, they had the good luck to meet Great Sail and his family paddling inland to their wintering grounds; Great Sail promised to look after the two men left in camp. At Keenees's village, they bartered gunpowder and shot for a plentiful supply of corn, but freezing rain and high winds kept them stormbound for more than a day. On the 16th, with their leaky canoe almost beyond repair, they made a desperate dash to Cuthbertson's trading post across the icy bay; Cuthbertson revived them with chocolate, repaired their canoe and provided two men, and a gallon of liquor, to see them safely back to the Carrying Place camp. Here they found Vincall and McEwen well fed on ducks and corn provided by Great Sail and his sons. At dinnertime the following day, two Rangers arrived with the promised horse and a feast of brandy, wine, tea, sugar, pork and bread. The next morning, with three native guides, they started their march south on the Toronto Carrying Place, and arrived at St. John's house on the Humber River about four o'clock in the afternoon on October 19. The next day, they were reunited with Simcoe and the rest of the expedition in York.

PILKINGTON'S MAP is the most detailed record of the Governor's return trip to York via the eastern trail, but surveyor Alexander Aitken kept a sketchy personal diary. On October 11, after noting the departure of Macdonell, Givins and the lame man headed for the "old landing place" to wait for a horse to be sent from York, Aitken writes:

His Excellency with the rest of the Party set out thro the woods to the last mentioned place [York]

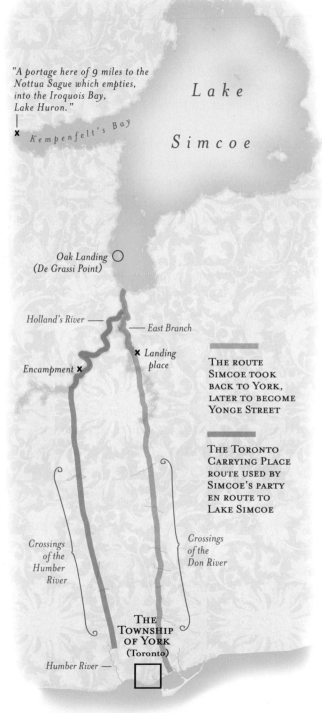

"A portage here of 9 miles to the Nottua Sague which empties, into the Iroquois Bay, Lake Huron."

Lake Simcoe

Kempenfelt's Bay

Oak Landing (De Grassi Point)

Holland's River

East Branch

Landing place

Encampment

THE ROUTE SIMCOE TOOK BACK TO YORK, LATER TO BECOME YONGE STREET

THE TORONTO CARRYING PLACE ROUTE USED BY SIMCOE'S PARTY EN ROUTE TO LAKE SIMCOE

Crossings of the Humber River

Crossings of the Don River

THE TOWNSHIP OF YORK (Toronto)

Humber River

Based on Robert Pilkington's map, this details the southern portion of Governor Simcoe's trip from Lake Ontario through Lake Simcoe and on to Georgian Bay.

DAWN HUCK, BASED ON AN ORIGINAL DRAWN BY ROBERT PILKINGTON

and got about 2 ½ miles from the Landing &
encamped on the Bank of the East Branch of
Holland's River in a cedar swamp. Our general
course about S.S.E – a heavy Rain –

Oct. 12th. Set off at daylight & after missing the
Path several times breakfasted at a Brook distant
about six miles from our last night's encampment.
After Breakfast set out and travelled about six
miles further & encamped on a Branch of the
Humber.

Oct. 13th. Got on to a small Branch of the river
Don & breakfasted distant about four miles from
our last Encampment – passed a small Pond about
a mile and a quarter from where we set out from
after breakfast. Travelled six or 7 miles further
to another branch of the Don and encamped.

Oct. 14th. Breakfasted on a third Branch of the
Don about four miles from our last camp & about
a mile & half further crossed the 4th Concession
Line of the Township of York at the Road between
no. 20 & 21. Got to York before three o'clock.

Simcoe, however, told his wife a dramatically different story. In her diary, Elizabeth Simcoe says that it was "Old Sail" who advised the Governor to take the eastern route to avoid "the Swamp", and that:

… the Gov. set out with only two days' provisions
& the expectation of 5 days' march to bring them
to York. The Indians lost their way & when they
had Provisions for one day only, they knew not
where they were. The Gov. had recourse to a
Compass & at the close of the day they came on
a Surveyor's line & the next Morning saw Lake
Ontario. Its first appearance, Coll. Simcoe says,
was the most delightful sight at a time they were
in danger of starving & about 3 miles from York
they breakfasted on the remaining Provisions.

Had they remained in the woods another day it
was feared Jack Sharp [Snap] would have been
sacrificed to their hunger. He has been troublesome
enough on this excursion as his size was very un-
suitable to a Canoe, but he is a great favourite.

Simcoe's response to the difficulties of the journey was to order a straight, Roman-style road, Yonge Street, to be slashed through the virgin forest from the pine fort landing on the East Holland River to York. The 1794 survey for this crude thoroughfare, not cleared by the Queen's Rangers until the early winter of 1796, acted as a magnet that drew squatters, speculators and settlers away from the outlying areas, including the Humber River and Toronto Carrying Place.

Simcoe encouraged settlement by Mennonites and Quakers, in spite of their pacifist views, because they were honest and industrious, and runaway slaves from the American South found freedom in Upper Canada, the first jurisdiction

RON WOLF

Tiny predators, loggerhead shrikes once bred by the hundreds between Lake Ontario and Georgian Bay; indeed, Lake Simcoe was the territorial heartland for these "butcher birds" and it's likely that Governor Simcoe's party heard their atonal alarm "shriek" as the birds gathered prior to migration. Today, loggerhead shrikes are endangered. Despite a variety of breeding and reintroduction programs, there are only an estimated thirty breeding pairs in Ontario; one of three core breeding areas is just northeast of Lake Simcoe.

Painted in 1804, this colourful depiction of Fort York, by artist Elizabeth Frances Hale, masks its shabby state.

in the British Empire to initiate the abolition of slavery. Infuriating American slave-owners must have delighted Simcoe, whose obsession with the imminence of American invasion was utterly at odds with the British government's policy of appeasement; to the English monarchy, the threat of American Republicanism paled against the war with Revolutionary France across the English Channel.

Apart from Fort York, a shabby, timber blockhouse surrounded by round log huts for the Rangers, no plans were approved for arsenals and fortifications, military posts or naval shipyards on the Great Lakes, and the roads, rutted wagon trails through the forest, were impassable during spring thaws and autumn rains. Muddy York, a straggling waterfront settlement of squat, log homes, taverns and workshops, each with a stable for livestock, a kitchen garden, and a chicken coop or pigsty, was a product of British parsimony and neglect; there was no church or schoolhouse, and the building planned for the Legislative Assembly looked like a warehouse.

In 1795, Mr. St. John, having toyed with the idea of relocating from the Humber River to the York waterfront, moved west instead to Ancaster, a village close to Joseph Brant and Rousseaux's Six Nations relatives. The next year, after barely four years in Upper Canada, Governor Simcoe was granted a leave of absence to return to England to recover his health; he did not return to Canada and resigned in 1798.

Anger and depression may have played a role in the mysterious chronic illness, variously described as gout, neuralgia, migraine, biliousness and malaria, that frequently made Simcoe bad-tempered, or an invalid. Tall, strong – he had walked across Upper Canada from Fort Niagara to Fort Detroit – Simcoe was courteous and hospitable to visiting dignitaries, but had no time for fancy dress balls, bureaucratic routine or the petty intrigues of colonial politics. His plans had been frustrated at every turn. He found it painful to justify to the Algonquian people the surrender to the United States of their ancestral lands, and he had raised doubts about the legitimacy of the 1787 Toronto Purchase of Mississauga lands.

Elizabeth Simcoe responded to her new home with enthusiasm, energy and curiosity. Well educated – she spoke French and Italian, and showed botanical expertise in identifying native plants – she sketched in pencil and painted scenic landscapes in watercolours. She found the Ojibwe "extremely handsome & have a superior air to any I have seen … when the Indians speak their air & action is more like that of Greek or Roman Orators than of Modern Nations. They have a great deal of impressive action & look like figures painted by the Old Masters."

She admired the Mississaugas' "ease & composure" in paddling their birchbark canoes: "I always wish to conduct a Canoe myself when I see them manage it with such dexterity and grace."

The Simcoe summer home, Castle Frank, was drawn by Elizabeth Simcoe in her diary.

No gentlewoman of Mrs. Simcoe's social position would be allowed to paddle, but, seated under an awning, she was toured around Toronto Harbour in a huge freight canoe given to the Simcoes by the North West Company. Elizabeth watched a Mississauga woman gum the canoe: "She held a piece of pitch in her hand & melted it by applying a piece of burning wood. Her figure was perfectly wild & witchlike & a little fire with her kettle on it by her side, in a stormy dark day the waves roaring on the beach near where she stood formed a scene very wildly picturesque."

Storms, sunshine or bitter cold, Elizabeth went for long walks, boat trips, and, in winter,

Between L a Lake Huron & Lake Simcoe

Though she had not travelled with her husband, Elizabeth Simcoe painted the McDonald Rapids, located on the Severn River between Sparrow Lake and Ragged Rapids, after an original done by Lieutenant Robert Pilkington.

sleigh rides, undeterred, or encouraged, by her pregnancy during her first winter at York. She reported on spearing salmon by torchlight at the mouth of the Humber River, and the great annual slaughter of passenger pigeons, but her favourite destination was Castle Frank, a pine house built in the style of a Greek temple on a bluff overlooking the Don River. Named for the Simcoes' infant son, Francis, it may have been intended as a model for York's future architecture, but it looked more like a rich woman's fantasy; Elizabeth had inherited a fortune, and in England the Simcoes lived in luxury on her estate in Devon. Her lively diary, sent home in installments to be read to their four young daughters, reveals none of the snobbery or arrogance of her class, but its weakness, for such an astute observer, is Elizabeth's lack of commentary on her closest companions: the quarrelsome little British colony at York. Was she being extremely discreet, given her husband's general unpopularity with the British government and his administrators, or did she save her gossip for private letters? Did she ever take tea on St. John's Creek with Rousseaux's wife, Margaret? Did she ignore that story, or did that meeting never happen?

Too bad that Governor Simcoe did not take his artist/journalist wife along on his expedition up the Toronto Carrying Place; for all the freedom Elizabeth was permitted, her presence would have contravened military protocol. She enjoyed riding horseback … and campfire pic-nics, with venison, duck, even raccoon – "like lamb if eaten with mint sauce" – roasted over the coals, but the adventure of living in a canvas tent on the edge of the wilderness, with small children, capricious servants, an often absent, sickly, preoccupied husband, and the obligations of her position as the "Governor's Lady", could be lonely and heartbreaking: "It is with pain I take up my pen to inform you of the loss we have sustained & the melancholy event of our losing poor little Katherine, one of the strongest, healthiest children you ever saw," Elizabeth writes to a friend, Mrs. Hunt, in May 1794. "She was the sweetest tempered pretty child imaginable, just beginning to talk & walk, & the suddenness of the event you may be sure shocked me inexpressibly." Katherine, born in Canada in 1793, and, from Elizabeth's description, the victim of a childhood infection, was buried in York.

Opposite: Late summer on the West Holland River

John Graves Simcoe: A Brief Tenure and Lasting Mark

THE TORONTO PURCHASE

IN 2002, the Canadian government and the Mississauga of the New Credit First Nation began to negotiate a land claim that includes most of the city of Toronto, the city of Vaughan to the north and rural King Township. The claim dates back to the Toronto Purchase of 1787, when Indian Commissioner Sir John Johnson persuaded three Mississauga chiefs, Wabakinine, Neace and Pakquan, to surrender the Mississaugas' title to all the land along the Toronto Carrying Place. According to Nathaniel Lines, the interpreter at the meeting, Johnson showed the chiefs a "Blank Deed". It did not describe the boundaries or the quantity of the land surrendered, and the chiefs' signatures, with their totems, were on bits of paper pasted on to the document. In exchange, the Mississauga received guns, ammunition and tobacco, barrels of flour and pork, brass kettles, hoes, blankets, bolts of linen, serge, calico, flannel and scarlet cloth, gartering,

In approving the Toronto Purchase in 1787, the Mississauga understood that they not only retained the right to fish or trap beaver, at right, but to move about their territory and camp where they pleased. The British, by contrast, believed they were buying the land outright. It took more than two centuries to settle the misunderstanding.

ribbons, beads, plain and laced hats, a broach and earbob for each of the 1,000 members of the Toronto band, and ninety-six gallons of rum.

What had Canada bought? To Sir John Johnson, the Toronto Purchase included ten square miles each at Toronto, Lake Simcoe and "the end of water communication to Lake Huron", and two to four miles on each side of the Carrying Place trail. For their part, the Mississauga drew the lakeshore boundaries between the Don and Humber Rivers, and "as far back a gunshot fired on the lakeshore could be heard in the interior." In *Sacred Feathers,* his biography of Mississauga Methodist missionary Peter Jones, Donald B. Smith argues that the Mississauga misunderstood the term "surrender":

There was nothing in the Mississaugas' traditions or experiences that enabled them even to imagine the private ownership of land and water by one person. Although a family could use a certain area as its

PETER ST. JOHN

DENNIS FAST

hunting and trapping ground, that land still belonged to every other band member, as much as to the supernatural beings and the natural world. The Mississauga had always regarded the presents the French supplied as a form of rent for the use of the land where the French posts stood and as a fee for the right to travel over their country. The Mississaugas understood that they had retained the right to 'encamp and fish where we pleased' throughout their territory. The British, in contrast, understood that they had extinguished the native title to the land that the Crown had obtained full proprietary rights.

As soon as survey crews started to stake out the boundaries of the Toronto Purchase, Mississauga protesters stopped them in the marsh east of the Don River and at Etobicoke Creek, west of the Humber. Alarmed by these altercations – the Mississauga were Britain's only loyal, peaceful ally among the rebellious Algonquin nations of the Great Lakes – Governor

Sir Guy Carleton, Lord Dorchester, investigated the circumstances of the Toronto Purchase. He concluded that the "proceedings are so informal and irregular as to invalidate and set aside the whole transaction."

Keeping the illegality secret, the Canadian government carried on with its surveys, road building and land sales to British and American immigrants. The Mississauga, treated as strangers in a Toronto they had inhabited for 100 years, shifted west to the Credit River. The British expected them to retreat north, to the "Indian Lands" of Lake Huron. Some likely did so, but while the Lake Ontario Mississauga had to fight off interlopers for control of their river mouth fisheries, they found new markets among the strangers for their fish, venison, berries, maple sugar, moccasins and baskets. York's waterfront marketplace was popular with everyone, and it was here, in August 1796, that Chief Wabakinine and his wife were murdered. *Sacred Feathers* gives the Mississaugas' memory of the tragedy:

Wabakinine had left the Credit River to sell salmon. The chief, his sister, and his wife camped at York, as the English now called Toronto, on the waterfront opposite Berry's tavern. The rest of the band had camped on the peninsula [now Toronto Islands]. Early in the evening a queen's ranger had offered Wabakinine's sister a dollar and some rum to sleep with him. Just before midnight the soldier, accompanied by two white settlers, came for her. Seeing the white men pull the chief's sister out from her resting spot under a canoe, Wabakinine's wife shook her husband to awaken him. Half asleep and half drunk, the big, muscular Indian staggered from under his canoe and in the darkness lunged awkwardly at the white men. The soldier grabbed a rock and repeatedly struck the Indian. Not yet finished, he kicked him in the chest and left him lying senseless on the ground. The men now seized Wabakinine's wife and viciously beat her. When the other Indians heard the wailing they rushed over from the peninsula, but the white men had left. Hurriedly they took the women and the chief to their campground, and early the next morning they left by canoe, returning to the Credit. The chief died that same day from his injuries, and his widow followed a day or so later.

The soldier, Charles McCuen, was arrested, but freed when no Mississauga attended court to testify against him. Authorities at York feared violent reprisals, but nothing came of the rumours. Powerless, ostracized, their numbers reduced to a few hundred, the Mississauga became so passive and acquiescent the Canadian government took the chance of asking them to approve a revised version of the invalid 1787 Toronto Purchase. In this formal deed, signed on August 1, 1805, the Mississauga surrendered 250,880 acres of land, including the Toronto Islands; in return, they received 10 shillings and the right to fish in Etobicoke Creek. Their request for presents was ignored.

The Mississauga clung to their old campsites until 1826, when the Methodists, with government assistance, built a model agricultural village on the Credit River for their dynamic young preacher, Peter Jones, and his converts. At last, in 1847, the Six Nations generously offered the Mississauga 6,000 acres of their own land north of Lake Erie near the present town of Hagersville.

On May 29, 2010 nearly two-thirds of the band members eligible to vote accepted a $145 million settlement from the Indian Claims Commission. Interest from the money, invesed in a trust fund intended to last at least one hundred years, will finance education and economic development, including the potential purchase of property in Toronto. Each of the 1,800 band members receives $20,000.

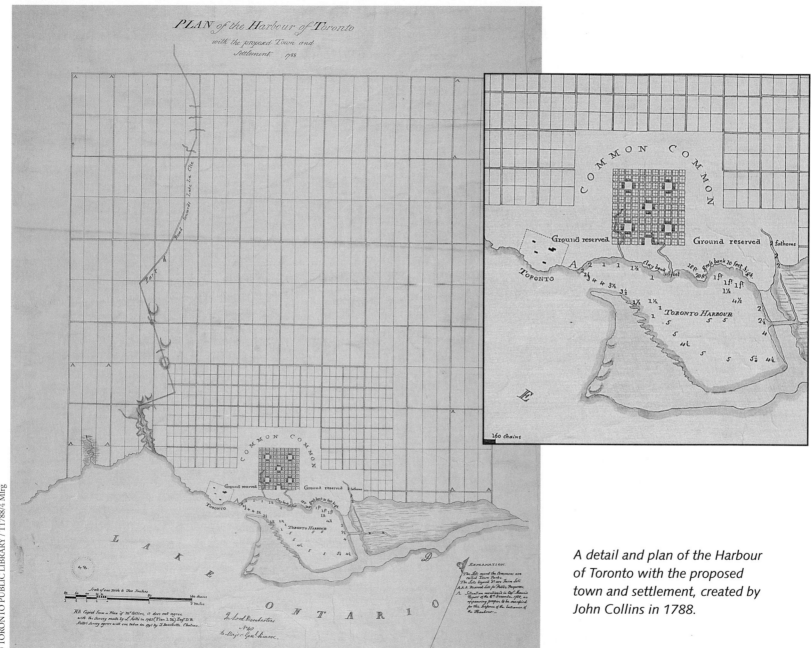

A detail and plan of the Harbour of Toronto with the proposed town and settlement, created by John Collins in 1788.

Dreams of England

On the Humber

"Toronto Coffee House" –

William Cooper begs leave to acquaint his friends

and the public that he has erected a large

and convenient stable on his own lot opposite

the Toronto Coffee House.

The rebuilt King's Mill on the Humber was drawn in 1878 for The Canadian Illustrated News.

T RAVELLERS WILL meet with genteel and comfortable accommodation at the above house, and their horses will be carefully attended to.

He has just received from New York a large supply of the best wines, brandy, Hollands, shrub, fresh lime juice, London porter, oysters, anchovies, red herrings, Devonshire, Navy and Cavis sauces, segars, pipes and tobacco. He has also received a very general assortment of groceries and dry goods, which he will sell cheap for cash or exchange for country produce.
—Upper Canada Gazette, *November 1802.*

A brash young Englishman, William Cooper claimed to have built the first house in York in 1793. In 1798, he opened a school in his home to teach reading, writing, arithmetic and English grammar to the sons of the local gentry. Within two years, he had become an auctioneer, coroner and usher of the Court of King's Bench; on Sundays he read the Anglican service in the Legislative Assembly Building. By 1806, Cooper had acquired 700 acres of land to build a grist mill and sawmill where the new western road, Dundas Street, crossed the Humber River at the Toronto Carrying Place. Cooper's Mill was one of the first to be built on the Humber since Simcoe's King's Mill in 1794. Through mismanagement or lack of business, the King's Mill had been abandoned in 1799. It burned to the ground in 1803 and was rebuilt, under new management, the following year. The King's Mill's closest customer was John Dennis, a master shipwright who built a variety of boats at the mouth of the Humber River between 1796 and 1801.

During this period, Dennis acquired for his family a vast tract of land east of the Carrying Place and north of Black Creek, an area, though now industrialized, that is still known as Mount Dennis.

However, any English hope of establishing a landed aristocracy in Upper Canada vanished before an onslaught of rebellious immigrants: Americans with democratic views, famished Irish, Scots evicted from their crofts, and British workers fleeing England's dark, satanic mills. Yet York's colonial administrators routinely rewarded military officers, civil servants, friends, speculators and, of course, themselves, with thousands of acres of virgin forest and swamp. These wilderness estates, bordered by Crown lands reserved for logging, the army and the Church of England, played an unexpected role in the American capture of York on April 27, 1813.

The United States and Britain had been at war since June 1812 (see page 143), and the U.S. Navy was threatening to drive British ships from the Great Lakes, yet Britain did nothing to fortify its defenceless little capital. "Only six hundred white men, including the militia and dockyard workers, were available to resist invasion," Edwin Guillet writes in *Early Life in Upper Canada*. "Even

The yacht Toronto, *in 1810*

this small body of defenders would have been 180 fewer if a detachment of the 8th Regiment, on the march from Kingston to Fort George, had not luckily halted at York the day before the attack; while the guns which protected the fortifications were merely three old French 24-pounders, captured in 1760 and all but buried in the earth."

On the morning of April 27, three U.S. warships and an armada of armed schooners blockaded the harbour. The gunships bombarded Fort York while a fleet of rowboats ferried 1,700 U.S. soldiers towards the shore.

"The landing place of the invader was just within the curve of the Humber Bay, far to the west, where Queen Street now skirts the beach for a short distance and then emerges on it," writes historian Henry Scadding. "The intention had been to land more to the eastward, but the vessels containing the hostile force were driven westward by the winds. The debarkation was opposed by a handful of Indians, under Major Givins. The Glengarry Fencibles had been dispatched to aid in this service, but, attempting to approach the spot by a back road, they lost their way."

The Fencibles could not have prevented the Americans from swarming ashore near Jean-Baptiste Rousseaux's old homestead at the end of the Toronto Carrying Place, then rushing along the only road through dense woods towards Fort York. York's militia, the 8th Regiment, and an assortment of other troops, commanded by Upper Canada's lieutenant-governor, General Sir Roger Sheaffe, put up a short, sharp fight in the bush, suffering serious casualties, before retreating into the town. As Sheaffe abandoned Fort York, he ordered a slow fuse to be lit to the gunpowder magazine. Timed to allow his men to get away safely, the smouldering fuse was a trap for the advancing Americans; almost as soon as they occupied the ground, the gunpowder exploded in a fiery hail of rocks, debris, ammunition and mangled bodies. Fifty-two American soldiers, among them General Zebulon Pike, were killed, another 180 were wounded.

In York, Sheaffe continued his scorched earth policy, burning everything of value to the enemy, including a warship, the *Isaac Brock*. He and his British troops then scurried east down the road to Kingston, destroying York's bridge over the Don River as a precaution. The officers of Upper Canada's civilian militia, with almost all of their men taken prisoner, were left with the humiliating duty of surrendering to the enemy. The American troops and local thugs looted and vandalized homes and public buildings; on May 1, the Legislative Assembly buildings were set on fire. The next day, the invaders rowed back to their ships; they sailed away a week later.

THE WAR brought prosperity to William Cooper. The demand for local lumber and flour enabled him to buy a rival's grist and sawmill on the west bank of the river, and by the time the war ended in December 1814, he had added a store, a forty-acre farm and a house with a fireplace in every room. In 1817, Cooper opened an inn with a tavern for his customers, and built a wharf and warehouse on the lakeshore in York to export his surplus flour and the potash, pork and farm produce he took in trade at his store.

The rebuilding of York in timber and brick, and a rush of immigrants who cleared the land and planted wheat, created a boom in the milling industry; new mills began leapfrogging up the Humber River from the King's Mill to the distant hamlet of Laskay on the Oak Ridges Moraine. Many were small, local operations, but the merchant millers, wealthy and well-connected

The village of York, fledgling capital of Upper Canada, as painted by Elizabeth Hale in 1804.

Charles and William Wadsworth's stately mill stood on the west side of the Humber River.

enough to acquire hundreds of acres of timber land and the money to build a mill, with its necessary distillery, inn, store and stables, were attracted by the opportunity to play the role of English country squire. When Canadian-born William Gamble bought the King's Mill in 1835, he renamed it Milton Mills for an English village, and Charles and William Wadsworth called their site Weston for their home in Somerset. The mill owners built grand houses of brick or stone on hills, with orchards, flower gardens and sweeping views of the valley, while shanty towns of coopers, blacksmiths, tanners, teamsters and other tradesmen sprang up around their mills.

The scene was medieval: a castle on a hill; a ramshackle wooden mill house, battered by spring floods and ice jams; smoke from a blacksmith's forge curling into the air as he shoed a horse or fashioned tools; lines of heavy wagons, some drawn by oxen, plodding to and fro along the dirt road; men dressed in homespun and flannel, their big boots made by a local tanner, women wrapped in long, loose calico dresses, wearing aprons. The air smelled of smoke, manure, fresh-sawn lumber and, at mealtimes, bread hot from the oven. Beneath the sounds of human voices and grinding millstones, the river murmured and gurgled as it eddied into a millrace or rippled over a log dam.

These people were not peasants. They were free to go where they wished, and they could avoid paying exorbitant prices at the mill owner's store by walking into York. Many were educated. In Weston, Captain John Pirritte, a graduate of Edinburgh University, ran a school in part of his small house. Later, a pharmacist, Dr. John Banks, taught reading, writing, arithmetic and drawing; his wife taught music, French, knitting and crocheting. Churches were the spiritual and social centres of the hamlets.

However, as long as Upper Canada was a colony, the common people had little political power. The masters of the mills, appointed by the governor as magistrates, justices of the peace and municipal inspectors, could reward or punish their labourers, tradesmen and the farmers whose grain they ground into flour. Miller John Scarlett retained his post as chief clerk in the inspector general's department, and they all served on the boards of churches, insurance companies and the banks that loaned them money. If a miller bought a commission in the militia, he might call himself "Colonel" or "Major", and wear a uniform, but if he were too pretentious, he was ridiculed as "Count" or "Pope". Living beyond their means, William Gamble, his brother John, and their business partner upstream on the Humber River, miller Thomas Fisher, were all bankrupted by the costs of rebuilding their mills after the fires and floods, and by the loss of export markets to American flour.

THE MODEL of gentlemanly deportment for his *nouveau riche* neighbours was a bi-cultural French Canadian, James Baby: Baby had Anglicized his given name, Jacques, but pronounced his surname with a soft French "ah". In 1815, Baby, a fifty-two-year-old widower with six young children, had acquired the beautiful promontory on the Humber River where the Iroquois village of Teiaiagon had once stood. His country estate had no vulgar mills, smithies or taverns, although they could be seen downriver. Baby lived on revenue from land speculation, and the generosity of a British government grateful for the loyalty of an old Quebec merchant family.

Baby's dignified bearing and genteel manners concealed that fact that he was the son of a tough frontier fur trader, Jacques Dupéront Baby.

James Baby, speaker of the Legislative Council of Upper Canada, 1826.

During the 1750s, Jacques, Louis and Antoine Baby had established a trading post at the little French outpost, Detroit; a fourth brother, François, managed the family business in Montreal. After the British conquest of Quebec in 1759, Baby *frères* transferred their European business from Paris to London; when James was born in Detroit in August 1763, at the height of Pontiac's siege, the Babys were firmly allied with the British. During the American Revolutionary War, the Babys' influence with their native customers was still strong enough to help keep them allied with Britain, and after Detroit was surrendered to the Americans, the Babys moved across the river to the village of Sandwich in Upper Canada.

In 1792, to everyone's amazement, Lieutenant-Governor John Graves Simcoe appointed inexperienced young James Baby, not yet thirty, to Upper Canada's all-powerful Legislative Council as lieutenant for the County of Kent.

The following year, Baby was made judge of the Surrogate Court of the Western District: he had been educated, in French, in Quebec, and legal training was not required for a judicial appointment in Upper Canada. In return, Baby organized the 1st Kent Militia and commanded it during the War of 1812, sharing in the British defeat at Moraviantown in 1813. During the war, American troops robbed and vandalized his home and farm in Sandwich, and his wife Elizabeth died of fever.

mouth of the Humber, Lake Ontario.
Sep? 18. 1831. JHMS —

A bridge at the mouth of the Humber River, painted in the English landscape tradition by James Bucknall

Denounced by his critics as a toady and greedy office seeker, James Baby was the only man in the government of Upper Canada who could negotiate in French with Lower Canada, where his uncle François, *un grand seigneur,* was part of the governor's inner circle. Baby was also a Western Canadian, a genuine representative of the scattered community of traders and voyageurs who, for generations, had established their families along the Detroit and St. Clair Rivers, and on Lake Huron at Michilimackinac and Sault Ste. Marie. By August 1814, these Canadians, with a few British soldiers, a young naval officer, and hundreds of Great Lakes Algonquin warriors, had driven the Americans off Lake Huron in a dramatic contest of strength and skill.

Shown being paddled across Lake Simcoe, these "Gentleman on their Travels" were painted by Henry B. Martin in 1832.

Lakeshore Boulevard looking southwest from east of the Humber River, as drawn by William J. Thompson.

The rocky shoreline of what is now Michigan's Upper Peninsula was well known to the sailors and soldiers who fought on both sides during the War of 1812. Today, this stretch of shore lies near a town named for its limestone boulders: Port Dolomite.

The War of 1812

When canoe courier Toussaint Pothier
brought the news of war with the United States
to St. Joseph's Island on July 3, 1812,
it came as no surprise to the traders, settlers and
soldiers of this isolated British outpost,
which guarded the Sault Ste. Marie rapids.

From the Loyal and Patriotic Society of Upper Canada, the "Upper Canada Preserved" medal was intended for veterans of the War of 1812.

A LL SPRING, the Montreal-based North West Company, the largest of the many outfits that used St. Joseph's Island as a base en route to Lake Superior, the Great Plains and the Pacific Ocean, had been stockpiling provisions, arms and ammunition and emptying its storehouses of furs. Then, suddenly, a fleet of canoes bearing more than 300 native warriors from south of Lake Superior descended on the little settlement; their leader, Indian agent Robert Dickson, had been alerted to the possibility of an American invasion by a secret letter from the British commander in Upper Canada, Major-General Isaac Brock.

Captain Charles Roberts, the officer in charge of St. Joseph's decrepit garrison, was grateful for the reinforcements; his only troops, forty-four men of the 10th Veterans' Battalion, were, in his opinion "so debilitated and worn down buy unconquerable drunkenness that neither fear of punishment, the love of fame or the honour of their Country can animate them to extraordinary exertions." Roberts himself, only forty, suffered from the disabling effects of a fever he had contracted while serving in the West Indies. If the Northwest was to be saved for Britain, it would have to be done by the native warriors and the Canadians.

Within days, 180 eager voyageurs, traders and clerks had formed themselves into a volunteer militia they called the Michigan Fencibles. Their quartermaster was Robert Livingston, a St. Joseph's Island trader and interpreter with the Indian Department. During the coming battle for Lake Huron, Livingston would turn the Nottawasaga River and Nine Mile Portage into a vital link with York and the supply road to eastern Canada. Like many of his neighbours, Livingston had married an Ojibwe, Amudwagewumaquait, a descendant, perhaps, of Alexander Henry's benefactor, Wa'wa'tam, or of one of the Ojibwe warriors who tried to kill Henry after the slaughter of the British garrison at Michilimackinac in 1763. Henry, now seventy-five, was a patriarch of Montreal's wealthy fur traders, but Michilimackinac, a prize won by the Americans in their War of Independence from Britain, was occupied by the U.S. Army.

Where was the U.S. Army in the summer of 1812? As the hot July days passed, St. Joseph's defenders peered anxiously across the lake towards Michilimackinac, as the British called what the Ojibwe knew as Mitchi-makinak, "Great Turtle Island" and Americans know today as Mackinac Island. (Confusingly, the original incarnation of Fort Michilimackinac, built about 1715, had been located on the nearby mainland.)

Michilimackinac was only forty miles southwest of St. Joseph's, but no warships' sails loomed on the horizon, and visitors reported business as usual at the trading posts that lined the beach below the fort: no gunboats were moored at the wharfs or cannon mounted on the bluffs, no soldiers were pouring in to reinforce the sixty-man garrison. Had the war been called off?

Not for Captain Roberts and the Canadians. Their combined force of native warriors, Michigan Fencibles and 10th Veterans outnumbered the Americans nearly ten to one, and they were hot to fight. When Roberts received a note from General Brock on July 15, advising him to "adopt the most prudent measures either of offense or defense which circumstance permit", his armada was ready to sail the next morning. The flagship, the North West Company's schooner *Caledonia*, carried two small cannon and the 10th Veterans, spruced up in their scarlet uniforms. The Michigan Fencibles, with Robert Livingston in the vanguard, followed in ten bateaux, surrounded by seventy bark canoes filled with Ojibwe, Odawa, Winnebago, Menominee and Nakota warriors in war paint and feathers.

The eastern sky was brightening as they landed on the narrow beach on Michilimackinac's northern shore, hidden from the fort by the thickly wooded hump of rock that formed the turtle's back. Not a sentry was to be seen, and they had encountered only one scout, a friendly trader, Michael Dousman,

A Grenadier private of the Royal Newfoundland Fencibles, by R. J. Marrion. The Newfoundland regiment joined the Royal Artillery during the War of 1812.

This view of Michilimackinac, with the turtle's back in the distance,
was painted by Richard Dillion Jr. in 1813.

whom they had apprehended in the middle of the channel paddling towards St. Joseph's for news. War? Dousman was astonished; no one on Michilimackinac knew that the United States was at war.

Silently, the little army filed along the single forest path leading to the fort, barely three miles away. The sun rose, and the garrison slept on. As the front ranks surrounded the old wooden palisade, Dousman and a detail of Veterans roused the civilians living on the beach below and herded them into an abandoned distillery. Only then did the army surgeon, Sylvester Day, who lived in the village, escape to the fort to raise the alarm.

The fort's commander, Lieutenant Porter Hanks, rallied his sixty men to their posts, but it was too late; this armed rabble of wild men and derelicts had even managed to mount a cannon on a hillock with a clear shot into his palisade. Retreat was impossible, and resistance would be suicide. Surrender was humiliating, but no more humiliating than his own ignorance. Without a shot being fired, Lieutenant Hanks surrendered the fort at 11 a.m. on July 17, 1812. As prisoners of war, he and his troops would be returned to the United States, on condition that they did not engage in combat unless exchanged for British prisoners. If the villagers swore an oath of allegiance to Britain, they could retain their homes and property; if not, they had a month to leave. The triumphant heroes of this bloodless invasion helped themselves to the U.S. Army's ample

stores of furs, guns, blankets, flour, wines and whisky, and the British flag flew once more over Michilimackinac.

The Americans did not forgive this insult to their pride, and their ambition to drive the British out of North America, but the British left the defence of their tiny garrison to the native warriors and Canadians; the only ships on Lake Huron, *Caledonia* and *Nancy*, belonged to the North West Company. These fast, lightweight schooners, designed to freight the company's furs, trade goods and provisions between its posts at Sandwich, a Loyalist settlement at the mouth of the Detroit River, and St. Joseph's Island, supplied the garrison as well. They were no match for American gunboats.

By October 1813, the Nottawasaga River, Nine Mile Portage and Yonge Street had become the only route the desperate British army could use to save its Michilimackinac outpost from starvation or surrender. The *Nancy* was its only ship; a month earlier, the *Caledonia,* captured by the Americans on Lake Erie and refitted as part of a newly built U.S. Navy, had helped the Americans destroy the entire British fleet on the lake.

The *Nancy* had narrowly escaped. The schooner's young captain, Alexander Macintosh, having heard nothing of the naval disaster, set sail from Michilimackinac in early October carrying several passengers and a cargo of furs for the North West Company post at Sandwich. When Macintosh had left Sandwich in the spring,

Detroit, which had been captured by General Brock the past August, had been securely in British hands. Yet, as he steered the *Nancy* into the swift, southward current of the St. Clair River, he sent two crewmen ashore to get news. It was terrible; the British army had abandoned all its Lake Erie forts, including Detroit, and been slaughtered on its retreat north. The *Nancy* was sailing into the arms of the enemy.

Macintosh turned his schooner's bow up-river, towards the safety of Lake Huron and Michilimackinac, but the north wind that had blown the *Nancy* into the river prevented her from sailing out. Her passengers disembarked, preferring to take their chances ashore, and were captured without harm by a group of American militia. An officer, waving a white flag, demanded the *Nancy's* surrender.

Prepared to blow up his ship rather than see her fall into enemy hands, Macintosh stalled for time. By nightfall, the north wind had died, and at daybreak, a south breeze ruffling the *Nancy's* sails convinced the crew that if they fought off their attackers, the wind would carry them up-river to safety. Macintosh aimed the *Nancy's* two small cannon towards the American troops, and after a short, sharp exchange of gunfire, they retreated. The *Nancy* reached Lake Huron with only a few bullet holes in her sails, but her real fight lay ahead. October storms, with gusts of hail and sleet, threatened to swamp her or smash her against the lake's desolate western shore.

Nine days later, the battered little schooner, her sails and rigging in shreds, her exhausted crew starving, dropped anchor at Michilimackinac.

The worst of the bad news the *Nancy* bore was her empty hold; the garrison, down to their last barrels of salt meat and flour, had expected her to return from Sandwich laden with provisions to see them through six months of winter. The new commander, Captain Richard Bullock, had been on the lake for barely three months. He had no orders to evacuate, and it would be weeks before a messenger sent to headquarters at Fort York returned. The *Nancy* was in dry dock, and all canoe routes to the east were freezing over.

Belatedly, Britain decided to defend and reinforce its isolated northern outpost. As Canada's governor, Sir George Prevost, expressed it: "The Island and Fort of Michilimackinac is of the first importance, as tending to promote our Indian connexion and secure them in our interest; its geographical position is admirable; its influence extends and is felt amongst the Indian tribes to New Orleans and the Pacific Ocean; vast tracts of country look to it for protection and supplies; and it gives security to the great trading establishments of the North-west and Hudson's Bay Companies …"

Opposite: Though fired upon by U.S. troops, and beset by autumn storms, the Nancy, *an eighty-foot schooner, was a thing of beauty on the Great Lakes.*

NORTH WEST COMPANY partners were among Prevost's closest advisors; they had been using Yonge Street as a trade route between Lake Ontario and Lake Simcoe for many years, and Alexander Henry had a vivid memory of crossing the Nine Mile Portage, the logical choice for a military expedition to relieve Fort Mackinac. Surveyor-General Samuel Wilmot recommended it, believing that twelve men could widen the path into a wagon road within ten days. The road was opened in January 1814.

Thirty shipwrights and workmen from the Royal Navy shipyard at Kingston were the first to cross it; years earlier, their foreman, John Dennis, had given up his own shipyard at the mouth of the Humber River to work for the navy. Their task, in the cold and the snow, was to build twenty-nine flat-bottomed bateaux big and sturdy enough to carry tons of supplies and 170 soldiers and seamen across Lake Huron as soon as the ice went out.

First, they had to chop down the trees and saw the boards. The clearing they made among the pines on a high bluff overlooking Willow Creek, a winding tributary of the Nottawasaga River, became a busy military campground when the troops arrived in March, half-frozen and footsore. They had marched from army headquarters at Kingston to Fort York, then up Yonge Street and across Lake

Replicas of the bateaux (as the French named these flat-bottomed boats) can be seen today at Historic Fort Willow.

Simcoe's windswept ice to the bottom of Kempenfelt Bay.

Lieutenant-Colonel Robert McDouall of the Glengarry Fencibles had under his command one officer and ten gunners of the Royal Artillery, 138 officers and men of the Royal Newfoundland Regiment and one officer and twenty seamen from the Royal Navy. The woods rang with the sound of axes and hammers as the men built a compound of huts, a storehouse, a blockhouse and rough fortifications. If Mackinac fell, Fort

BARRY WALLACE

Willow, as it was later named, would become Upper Canada's front line of defense against an American invasion from the north. Plans were made to stock it as a permanent depot.

The most important member of the McDouall expedition was the fur trader, Robert Livingston. Since the outbreak of war, Livingston, who had been promoted to lieutenant, had acted for the British army as a recruiter among the native tribes and a courier between Mackinac Island, Fort York and military posts on the Niagara frontier. Only six months earlier, he had been severely wounded in a skirmish. "By those wounds he is in a great measure deprived of the Sight of his right eye by the blow of a Tomahawk, which he received from the Inimical Indians," he wrote in a petition for a pension. "Is also deprived of the Natural use of his right arm owing to the Stab of a Spear which he received on his Shoulder, and was also wounded in the head, the fourth wound is a musket-ball in his left thigh, which remains unextracted."

Scarred as he was, Livingston was still the best man to guide the McDouall Expedition. Routinely travelling hundreds of miles by canoe, or on snowshoes in winter, Livingston knew every cove and reef on the lake's north shore, a safe channel sheltered from the wind by a string of rocky islands, and he was on excellent terms with the people who lived there.

Impatient to get a jump on the Americans, McDouall's troops loaded the bateaux and skidded them over the ice to frozen Willow Creek. On April 22nd, they embarked and chopped a channel through the ice until they were able to row into open water. Two days later, Lieutenant Andrew Bulger of the Royal Newfoundland Regiment wrote in a dispatch: "Encamped on the night of the 24th of April, in a most dismal spot, upon the north-eastern shore of Lake Huron; and, on the following morning, entered upon the attempt to cross the lake, covered, as it was, as far as the eye could reach, by fields of ice: through which, in almost constant and at times terrific storms, we succeeded, with the loss of only one boat, in effecting a passage a distance of nearly three hundred miles, arriving at Fort Mackinac on the 18th of May." The wrecked men had been rescued. In Robert Livingston's opinion, "If that Detachment arrived Safe it was owing to the vigilance of their conductor."

The British flag fluttered over the fort. No American ships were in sight, and the *Nancy*, refitted by her crew over the winter, bobbed at anchor in the harbour. The garrison, though healthy on a native diet of cornmeal and whitefish, was barefoot: McDouall, taking over command from Bullock, wrote an urgent order for 200 pairs of shoes and 400 pairs of American socks. However, the provisions so laboriously transported from Fort Willow did not begin to feed the hundreds of native warriors who had congregated to defend the island. McDouall needed another 400 barrels of flour and pork and ten casks of rum. HMS *Nancy*, conscripted into the Royal Navy, set sail for Nottawasaga Bay to start Livingston on his way to Fort York with McDouall's message, and to bring more stores from Fort Willow. Within nine days she returned safely with her cargo.

McDouall set about transforming the island into a fortress. The Royal Artillery, well stocked with ammunition and guns, including four heavy field guns, built a blockhouse on the hillock overlooking the fort and the harbour. "As the enemy might arrive in the night," Bulger writes, "the ordinary guards were augmented at sun-down, to one-third of the garrison, in addition to parties of Indians, who were stationed on the look-out, at various points. We had been joined by upwards of four hundred warriors of different tribes, some of whom had come from a remote distance beyond the lakes." On June 5, a grand war-council was held in the open air. Writes Bulger, "the Indians, from six to eight deep, were seated on the ground upon three sides of a square; while the Head Chiefs, one after the other, standing in front of their respective bands, delivered speeches of a highly satisfactory nature."

McDouall replied with a complimentary oration, concluding: "My Children: Happy are those warriors who rush into the fight and have justice on their side. You go forth to combat for the tombs of your forefathers and for those lands which ought now to afford shelter and sustenance to your wives and your children. May the Great Spirit give you strength and courage in so good a cause and crown you with victory in the day of battle."

But where was the enemy? June passed with no sign of an American ship on the lake. Then, early in July, news came that a small U.S fleet had been spotted among the islands west of Penetanguishene, searching in the wrong place for the British supply depot. Frustrated, their six ships sailed for St. Joseph's Island and Sault Ste. Marie, where they burned the vacated Fort St. Joseph and destroyed the fur traders' warehouses, wharfs and boats. On July 28, the long-expected visitors arrived off Michilimackinac: two U.S. warships, the *Lawrence* and *Niagara*, two armed schooners, the *Tigress* and *Scorpion*, and two gunboats, carrying in all 1,000 soldiers. They did not have the *Nancy* in tow; she was out on the lake, expected back any day loaded with supplies. McDouall sent Livingston in an express canoe to find the schooner and warn her captain to hide her as far as possible up the Nottawasaga River.

The island's defenders prepared for battle, but for seven days the American fleet hovered uncertainly around it. The broad beach below the British fort was the ideal place to land their assault troops, under cover of a naval bombardment, but the warships' guns could not be angled high enough to hit the fort or its blockhouse above, and their hot shells rained down on the settlement behind the beach, where some of the residents were American citizens. In fact, the largest building,

Fort Mackinac on Mackinac Island: Known as Michilimackinac by the British, it was renamed by the Americans following the War of 1812. Today, the fort is a National Historic Site, and sits atop slopes that are still densely forested.

the South West Company's warehouse and store, was owned by American fur trade magnate John Jacob Astor. Astor, who hated the war as much as his friend, Alexander Henry, would not be pleased to have his property destroyed by friendly fire.

On the morning of August 4, the American flotilla anchored off the island's north shore, opposite the sandy cove where Captain Roberts' 10th Veterans, native warriors and Canadians had landed to surprise the American garrison two years earlier. McDouall was waiting. Hidden in the dense forest on the hill behind the beach, out

of range of the U.S. Navy's guns, he had positioned 200 British regulars and Michigan Fencibles, with two field guns; 300 native warriors guarded his flanks. They watched, holding their fire, as the American troops, with six field guns, disembarked.

"Shortly after landing," Lieutenant Bulger writes, "the enemy's troops, preceded by their guns, having passed through a strip of wood, advanced directly towards us; and before many minutes had elapsed, the fire of their artillery was concentrated upon our position.

THE WAR OF 1812

153

A view of the Nottawasaga River from Lieutenant Miller Worsley's log blockhouse

"We occupied commanding ground; and, in front, were, in some degree, covered by a natural breastwork. At first, the fire of our guns was reserved; but a few rounds, in the nick of time, sufficed to cause a hasty retreat of the Americans to the wood, through which they had previously passed; and after nearly half and hour's firing, their artillery, also, drew off."

Repulsed, the U.S. troops attempted to make an end run around Bulger's left flank: "The Americans had not proceeded far into the wood when they were attacked, both in front and on their right, by a band of our Monomonie and other Indians. These warriors were, in a great measure, hidden by the trees, but 'the war-whoop' – their battle cry – resounded through the wood." With the warriors holding the line, McDouall made a surprise attack against the Americans on his right.

"Apprehending that they were about to be surrounded," says Bulger, "the American troops fell back in complete disorder, leaving their killed (including their second-in-command) as also many of their wounded, on the field – and, upon being closely pressed, continued to retreat to their shipping, under the guns of which they lost no time in re-embarking."

After retrieving their sixty-four dead and wounded under a flag of truce, the Americans sailed away, but McDouall knew they would not go far. Freeze-up would eventually force their ships off the lake, but that was months away, and even after the warriors and militia went home,

he could feed his garrison for barely three weeks. Where was the *Nancy*?

U.S. Navy Commander Arthur Sinclair thought he knew. An "intelligent prisoner" captured during their raids on the mainland had blabbed about a British supply depot at the mouth of the Nottawasaga River. As soon as Sinclair sent the Lawrence back to Detroit with his casualties and half his soldiers, he and his fleet would investigate Nottawasaga Bay.

August 13, 1814: HMS *Nancy* lies at anchor about two miles up the Nottawasaga River, concealed from the lake by sand dunes covered with scrub willow and pine. High on the riverbank behind, her crew pushes her small cannon into place in their hastily built log blockhouse. To defend her, the schooner's new captain, Lieutenant Miller Worsley of the Royal Navy, has twenty-two sailors, a surgeon, nine Canadian boatmen and, at best, two dozen Ojibwe warriors that Robert Livingston recruited from a local fishing camp. Just twenty-three, this is Worsley's first command. He has no idea what to expect. Has Michilimackinac fallen? Does the American fleet know where the *Nancy* is? He has had no news since Livingston hallooed him on the lake about ten days ago. Posted here only weeks before, Worsley knows nothing about Lake Huron, but he will learn. He knows his sailing master, the *Nancy's* former captain, Alexander Macintosh, outwitted the Americans on the St. Clair River by bravado and expert seamanship.

The wind is gentle, and as the slanting afternoon sun bathes its crescent beaches in golden light, three American ships enter Nottawasaga Bay: Commander Sinclair on *Niagara*, with twenty heavy guns, and armed schooners *Tigress* and *Scorpion*. The bay's shallow water prevents them from closing in on the river's mouth, but they have a clear view of the *Nancy's* hiding place. Sinclair sends a reconnaissance party ashore. Scrambling over the dunes, they spot the blockhouse and the schooner's masts among the trees.

The hull remnants of the Nancy, *displayed at the Wasaga Beach Visitors Centre*

Worsley watches the excited soldiers row back to their ship. He has time to surrender, or retreat to Fort Willow, but he is not afraid; as a midshipman, he took part in the battle of Trafalgar, and recently won his command by distinguishing himself in the capture of Fort Oswego on Lake Ontario. He and his men will stand their ground. Worsley runs a line of gunpowder from the blockhouse to a keg of ammunition in the *Nancy's* hold; he will blow her up rather than hand her over.

At 9 a.m. the next morning, August 14, the American guns open fire. Their thunder booms around the bay, but their shells explode harmlessly in the lake, or shatter the trees. By noon, the battle has reached a standoff. Sinclair has 450 soldiers on his ships, but he does not storm the deserted beach. There is no army of redcoats lining up to oppose him, no sign of a British depot, and the cannon fire from the blockhouse is feeble. Sinclair lands a rapid-fire howitzer on the dunes. For four hours, his howitzer rains hot shot on Worsley's little garrison. One sailor is killed, another wounded.

Two months later, Worsley writes to his father, "Finding my little crew were falling all around me, I immediately formed a resolution to blow up, which I did, made my escape with the rest of my little crew through the woods to the great astonishment of the enemy.

"We walked that night with our wounded and dying 36 miles before we came to any house. We lost everything we had except what we stood upright in."

High on the bank of the Notawasaga River, in the centre of this watercolour
by Alexander Cavalié Mercer, are the remains of Lieutenant Worsley's blockhouse.

A Hundred Years Peace; a century after the Treaty of Ghent in 1814,
artist Amedee Forestier imagined it this way.

While the surgeon tends to the wounded, Fort Willow, manned largely by storekeepers and boatmen, prepares for attack. Then comes startling news: the American fleet has vanished.

U.S. Navy Commander Sinclair, contemplating the smouldering ashes of the *Nancy* and her cargo, credited his own gunners with the fiery death of the last British ship on the lake, but he was uneasy at finding no corpses in the ruins of the blockhouse; her defenders had escaped into the bush. Should he follow? Sinclair's "intelligent prisoner" had led him to believe that the British depot was forty-five miles inland, and that the winding, swampy Nottawasaga River was "dangerous and difficult." His soldiers, routed at Michilimackinac, had no stomach for another battle in an impenetrable forest swarming with native warriors.

"The Nautauwasauga is too narrow and over hung with bushes for a vessel to get up except by warping," Sinclair later reported, "which prevented my sending gunboats in. We saw a number of Indians skulking and occasionally firing across from the bank, it was in this way the only man we had touched was wounded." Instead, Sinclair ordered his two schooners, *Scorpion* and *Tigress*, "to blockade it closely until the season becomes too boisterous for Boat transportation." With the *Niagara* and the gunboats, Sinclair returned to Detroit.

With no harbour to protect them, the American schooners lay fully exposed to north winds sweeping down the bay, threatening to drive them onto the rocks and the sandbars. After riding out three violent storms, Lieutenant Daniel Turner, commander of both boats, disobeyed his orders; the *Scorpion* and *Tigress* sailed towards the shelter of the lake's north channel.

Fort Willow; August 24, 1814: Lieutenant Worsley and his little crew decide to risk a fast run across the lake to Michilimackinac. Two bateaux manned by eighteen seamen are loaded with barrels of flour and pork; Robert Livingston in his canoe will act as guide and scout. Each boat carries a gun in its bow and all the men are armed. Six days later, they enter the Detour, a narrow channel leading south from St. Joseph's Island. They have only forty miles to go. Then, with "great astonishment and regret", Worsley spies the *Scorpion* and *Tigress* ahead. The bateaux veer into a bay and their crews hide them on shore without being seen.

During the night, all the men crowd into the canoe and paddle silently past the sleeping schooners. The next day, they are greeted by the jubilant garrison at the fort. Worsley proposes to McDouall a joint force of sailors and soldiers to "cut out" the enemy ships "with every prospect of success". McDouall agrees, believing that clearing his lifeline to Fort Willow and saving the Northwest for Britain are worth the risk. The next evening, the first of September, Worsley's sailors and fifty volunteers from the Royal Newfoundland Regiment, in four bateaux, set off towards the Detour. On September 2, they camp. The next morning, Worsley, in Livingston's canoe, slips into the Detour to reconnoiter the enemy's position; the *Tigress* is anchored about six miles away, alone.

Worsley decides to attack at nightfall. His men, armed with pistols, daggers and boarding axes, outnumber the enemy two-to-one, and no one on board the *Tigress* seems to be keeping watch. As twilight deepens, the Newfoundlanders, in their scarlet jackets, the seamen in blue, row, with muffled oars, within range of the schooner's 24-pound gun. All is quiet. They are pulling within ten yards, circling the ship, when a watchman hails them; they make no reply. He sounds the alarm, and the schooner's big gun roars, but the British are scrambling up her sides. Three American sailors are thrown overboard and drowned; four are killed and five wounded before the *Tigress* surrenders. Two men of the British force are killed, and ten wounded.

Worsley learns from his prisoners that the *Scorpion* is about fifteen miles up the channel, too distant to have heard the gunfire. At daylight, his scouts report that she is sailing towards them. *The Tigress* lies in wait, with the American flag flying from her masthead. Her shackled captain and crew are packed off to Michilimackinac by canoe and bateau. On September 5, the *Scorpion* anchors two miles away and Worsley signals all is well. The Newfoundlanders, covered in American greatcoats, lie still on the deck or stay below.

On the morning of September 6, the *Tigress*, sailing with only a jib and foresail, bears down on the *Scorpion*. Nothing is amiss; the *Scorpion's* sailors are swabbing her decks. Worsley fires a shot across her bow and the Newfoundlanders dash to the railings. Raking *Scorpion's* decks with volleys of gunfire, they swarm aboard. The battle is over in minutes. With two men dead and four wounded, Turner surrenders.

Worsley writes to his father: "Thus you see after a series of hardships I have got two schooners, both finer vessels than the *Nancy* and have providentially escaped unhurt."

NOW MASTER of the lake, Worsley renamed his prizes HMS *Surprise* and *Confiance*. During the autumn, they sailed between Michilimackinac and Nottawasaga, carrying his prisoners to be escorted to Fort York, returning with flour, pork, rum, socks and shoes, plenty to keep the garrison comfortable over the winter. The native warriors were rewarded with flour, blankets, guns and ammunition, and the North West Company sent canoe brigades from Montreal to rebuild its trading post at Sault Ste. Marie.

The war ended on Christmas Day, 1814. The Treaty of Ghent called for "the mutual restoration of all the forts." In the spring, therefore, Britain gave the island back to the United States. When Robert McDouall heard the news, he was "penetrated with grief at the restoration of this fine island, a fortress built by nature for herself. Our negociators [sic], as usual, have been egregiously duped."

A watercolor of a corporal's house located on the portage between Lake Simcoe
and the Nottawasaga River, as painted by George Back.

FORT WILLOW
AND THE
NINE MILE PORTAGE

AS LONG as people travelled by canoe, boat, wagon, or on foot, the Nine Mile Portage remained a popular route connecting the Atlantic, Pacific and Arctic Oceans. At the end of August 1815, 140 destitute Scots refugees from Lord Selkirk's distant colony at Red River arrived at the North West Company's trading post at the mouth of the Nottawasaga River. Driven from their highland crofts by their laird, the Duchess of Sutherland, to make room for sheep, they had arrived at Red River in the spring of 1814 in the midst of an armed uprising of Métis buffalo hunters determined to destroy the colony. Having lost many of their kin to fever during their long voyage, and suffered through a hungry winter on Hudson Bay dependent on the niggardly charity of the Hudson's Bay Company's Fort Churchill, these highlanders had no loyalty to Lord Selkirk or to the company he represented. In the spring of 1815, they gladly accepted the rival North West Company's offer to transport them to Upper Canada, where they were promised 200 acres of land and provisions for a year. Soon after they had left Red River on their ten-week canoe journey, the Métis frightened away the remaining settlers and burned their houses.

Crossing the portage and Lake Simcoe to the little settlements on Yonge Street at Holland Landing and Newmarket, the "Selkirks", as the Red River Scots were called, found there was no free land; it had not yet been surveyed. Many families continued on south, but with the British building a naval base at Penetanguishene, and freighting tons of supplies from York to Fort Willow, there was plenty of paid work for those who remained. In the early summer of 1816, some of Selkirk's "mutineers", as he called them, may have helped transport the angry earl himself to meet his secret agent, Robert Livingston, at Nottawasaga.

Determined to rebuild and defend his ruined prairie colony, Selkirk recruited a private army of ninety mercenaries in Montreal, and hired Livingston, now Captain Livingston, to help organize and equip his expedition as far as Sault Ste. Marie. In January 1816, Livingston, with three companions, walked on snowshoes, in terrible weather, from Newmarket to "the Soo" to deliver Selkirk's instructions to Charles Ermatinger, a free trader who would provision the expedition on its long trip across Lake Superior; by March 1, Livingston had walked back to York.

Selkirk next asked him to blaze, in secret, the "French trading path" from Toronto to Nottawasaga, but Livingston replied that the Toronto Carrying Place could only be used by people on foot, carrying small canoes. In the spring, he had bateaux built for Selkirk's men at Holland Landing and the mouth of the Nottawasaga River, then arranged for wagons to haul their boats and baggage across the Nine Mile Portage. With Livingston as guide, the Selkirk expedition left Nottawasaga at the end of June. But instead of proceeding directly to Red River, Selkirk attacked and captured the North West Company's Fort William at the head of Lake Superior: it was his revenge for the murder in June of his colony's governor and twenty citizens by a band of Métis allied to the Nor'westers.

By the time the war between the Hudson's Bay Company and the Nor'westers was resolved by their merger in 1821, seventeen families of Selkirk's "mutineers" were taking up land in the new Township of West Gwillimbury, southwest of Lake Simcoe, an area known to this day as the Scotch Settlement. Among them was George Bannerman, the great-grandfather of a future Canadian prime minister, John George Diefenbaker.

Thomas Douglas, the Fifth Earl of Selkirk

LIBRARY AND ARCHIVES CANADA / C-001346

May 21, 1822: In a letter to Anthony Barclay, British representative on the International Boundary Commission, David Thompson outlined his plans to survey Lake Superior that summer. An astronomer, explorer and retired fur trader, Thompson had paddled from Montreal to the mouth of the Columbia River on the Pacific Ocean, located the source of the Mississippi River, and mapped much of the Hudson Bay watershed. Now, at fifty-two, Thompson was working with his American counterparts to draw the border between Canada and the United States:

The men for the voyage are engaged at the wages settled at New York: 14$ for the foreman and steersman, and 12$ to each middle man. The high

Canada Post commemorated David Thompson's legacy of surveying a century after his death with a stamp that was issued on June 5, 1957.

prices for expert men on the rapids of the Ottawa river, made it unreasonable for me to pass that way. The very difference in the price of one man's wages will pay the transport from York to Lake Simcoe, for those men could not be procured under 25$ per month, and I did not think myself authorized to part so far from my orders. And the two routes to Lake Huron are nearly equally eligible except the Ottawa has the advantage of preventing the desertion of men, but is far more dangerous.

Falls of Ste. Maries, 24 June, 1822: *My last letter was I believe dated the 9th June at Lake Simcoe, Natawasuaga Carrying Place … The person who had the contract for cartage had only one team of oxen, and those [he] harassed to death; and his time being almost expired, would make no exertions, it was the 4th day of June at 2 Pm before we got afloat in the brook; the next day by 7 Am we were in Lake Huron.*

Returning from Lake Superior in September, Thompson endured freezing, windy weather. On October 1, he left Sault Ste. Marie for home:

Very cold – two of my men who had gone down to the village and been drinking all night refused to embark; I could not afford at this season to wait 3 days for them to get sober. Therefore left them, and came on with 4 men; this month was still more stormy than September. These 3 years past have been remarkable for drought; frequent and long calms and very heavy gales of wind when they did happen. This year the waters have risen … and continued as if by some occult cause: the winds a constant gale mostly SSE often severe yet without extreme violence. Lake Huron proved as unpropitious as Lake Superior, and it was the 25 Oct. before we entered the Notawasuaga River. On the 26 we arrived in the evening at the carrying place, and Nov 1 at Holland Landing within 36 miles of York and here thank God our miseries found an end.

The next summer, Thompson took along a young Englishman, John J. Bigsby, on his survey of Rainy Lake and Lake of the Woods. Bigsby, an amateur geologist, was a keen observer, and in his memoir, *The Shoe and Canoe*, he describes the hilly countryside around Yonge Street as a picturesque vista of lakes and forests, with fine large farms on the flats, country inns and a little village, Newmarket, to the east. Crossing Lake Simcoe by boat, Bigsby was impressed by the ferocity of the black-flies, and beauty of Kempenfelt Bay's untouched forest. "We took up our abode near the bottom

View at Barrie, Kempenfeldt Bay, Lake Simcoe, was painted by George Russell Dartnell in 1841.

LIZ SAUL

WALKING INTO WILDERNESS: THE TORONTO CARRYING PLACE AND NINE MILE PORTAGE

of the bay in a lonely house, occasionally used as an inn by the few travellers. It was then kept by a respectable person named Johnson, who had a numerous family. Here commences a portage of nine miles to a small branch of the Notawasaga; and here we were detained for five days, during very stormy weather for most of the time."

Describing the house as clap-boarded, large and square, with "four sleeping rooms, partly in the roof, two good parlours, and a bed-chamber for guests of quality," Bigsby adds:

So new was the wood when the house was put together, or so hot are the summers in Kempenfelt Bay, that it had shrunk most grievously. The kitchen and the parlour might almost be called parts of a cage, so well were they ventilated. I also remember a round tub of a boat staked to the lake shore, and a little garden of herbs … A hundred yards or so inland begins the forest – a fragrant forest of firs, maple, beech, oak, and iron-wood – many of the trees from fifty to seventy feet high, without a branch. As there is no undergrowth, we may walk at our ease for miles on a soft carpet of last year's leaves.

At length we left Johnson's, to cross the portage – a broad, sandy opening in the woods. Near its lower end we found ourselves over-looking from a lofty bank a vast prospect of marsh and wood, stretching to the south thirty miles or more, and bounded eastward by a long range of blue hills. Not far from this escarpment there was a post for two soldiers, as a guard to any military stores that

might pass. An absurd tyranny was practiced even here. The stronger soldier was in the daily habit of chastising his comrade for supposed breaches of discipline. Being seldom visited, the weaker man had no present redress.

In this forbidding marsh, which, in South America, would have been peopled with serpents and alligators, we descended, and near a deserted building embarked in a stagnant creek, twenty feet broad, often quite benighted by trees and creeping plants.

We worked cautiously among fallen trees and loosened masses of earth for eight miles along the perpetual doublings of the creek, among inundated woods of alder, maple, willow and a few elm and ash. We entered the Notawasaga gladly from the north: it is large and long. We struck it, twenty-five miles from Lake Huron, thirty to forty yards broad, and running two miles an hour through grounds for the most part under water, with here and there mounds of slippery shining ooze, weedy mud, or even knolls of grass and trees. It has many sharp turns and long reaches, amid spots of exquisite woodland scenery. Here we often startled the busy wildfowl. As we descend, the river begins to have high banks, and it swells out into two pretty but small lakes, dotted with isles of marsh and willows, near the Rapids.

These Rapids are nine miles long. They only average three miles an hour, and are not rough,except then obstructed by rafts of fallen trees. Their smoothness may, in part, arise from the bed of the

Opposite: Still much as Bigsby found it in 1823, Minesing Swamp is recognized today as a provincially significant Area of Natural and Scientific Interest. Thousands of migrating birds stage here annually and several species of rare warblers are found.

river being of white clay or marl, which the soldiers of Penetanguishene use to clean their belts.

Below the Rapids the river assumes a steady width of 150 to 200 yards, with high scarps of sand, bearing groves of fir. It is now for several miles a truly fine river, the land about it dry and fertile, with some magnificent pines. We saw scarcely any living thing in the lower part of the river. Now and then we caught sight of a wild duck or solitary Indian, and of his canoe gliding under the shadow of high and umbrageous banks.

The Notawasaga discharges into Lake Huron between banks of drift-sand and shells, which, on the left, shelter the little trading-post of Mr. Robinson, while the other side has a thin grove of pines. There is a bar at the mouth: and, smooth as it was when I passed it, it is the seat of a raging surf when a high north-west wind prevails, and is the dread of all who travel in canoes.

'Huron! Chantons, le lac Huron!' cried our steersman. He then struck up the spirited and original air, which is married to the following simple words; and was well chorused by his comrades:

'Le premier jour de Mai
Je donnerais à m'amie
Une perdrix, oh, là! Qui vole, qui vie,
qui va là!
Une perdrix, oh, là! Volant dans les bois.

Le deuxième jour de Mai
Je donnerais à m'amie
Deux tourterelles, une perdrix, oh, là!
Qui vole, qui vie, qui va là!
Une perdrix, etc.'

Returning across the portage by wagon in the autumn, the Thompson expedition, accompanied by the American boundary commissioner's agent, Colonel Joseph Delafield, impressed their teenaged teamster, Tom Williams:

They travelled by their own beautiful bark canoes – two of them – one propelled by ten men, the other by eight, North West voyageurs. I never in my life saw such complete outfit for comfort in travelling as with this party. Their tents, when set up, impressed me as luxurious – everything to contribute to comfort and taste in such a life. I was also much interested in the members of the party – the commissioner [Thompson], his son and secretary, 'the Colonel,' a long, lank American, but a very interesting gentleman, and their three servants, besides the eighteen canoe-men, or voyageurs. No party or doing of the whole season interested me so much.

EARLY IN April 1825, the famous British explorer, Sir John Franklin, arrived in York to lead his second expedition to "the shores of the Polar Sea"; once again, Franklin was accompanied by naturalist Dr. John Richardson, and Lieutenant George Back. Compared to the extreme hardships of the western Arctic, where many of Franklin's first expedition

A scene painted by George Alexander Frazer: Sir John Franklin and his party find a quiet inlet to breakfast on the north shore of Lake Huron.

had perished, the first leg of this journey was unremarkable. Franklin writes: "From York we passed on to Lake Simcoe, in carts and other conveyances, halting for the night at the hospitable house of Mr. Robinson of Newmarket. We crossed Lake Simcoe in canoes and boats, and landed near the upper part of Kempenfeldt Bay, but not without being obliged to break our way through the ice for a short distance. A journey of nine miles, performed on foot, brought us to the River Nattawassaga, which we descended in a boat; and passing through a part of Lake Huron, arrived at Penetanguishene."

As the threat of war with the United States disappeared, and farming replaced fur as the mainstay of the economy, the Nine Mile Portage disappeared into farm lots, and a little town, Barrie, sprang up at the bottom of Kempenfelt Bay. When the railway line from York bypassed Nottawasaga

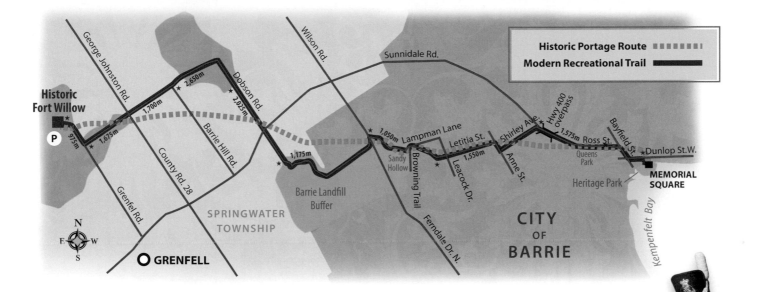

Historic Portage Route ▪▪▪▪▪▪▪▪
Modern Recreational Trail ▬▬▬▬

George Johnston Rd.
Wilson Rd.
Sunnidale Rd.
2,650 m
1,700 m
Dobson Rd.
2,025 m
Historic Fort Willow
975 m
1,675 m
Barrie Hill Rd.
County Rd. 28
1,175 m
1,050 m   Lampman Lane
Letitia St.
Shirley Ave.
Hwy 400 overpass
1,575 m   Ross St.
Bayfield St.
Dunlop St. W.
Sandy Hollow
Browning Trail
1,550 m
Leacock Dr.
Anne St.
Queens Park
Grenfel Rd.
MEMORIAL SQUARE
Heritage Park
Barrie Landfill Buffer
Ferndale Dr. N.
SPRINGWATER TOWNSHIP
CITY OF BARRIE
Kempenfelt Bay
○ GRENFELL

for a new harbour at Collingwood in 1855, the Nottawasaga swamp was left to hunters, trappers and loggers. Fort Willow fell into decay, but old timers like Reverend Thomas Williams had long memories, and stories to tell to their descendants.

In 1955, archaeologist Wilfrid Jury of the University of Western Ontario and a group of local residents, supported by the Barrie Chamber of Commerce, tramped through farm fields, woods and city streets mapping the route of the old portage. In 1959, Jury and his wife Elsie excavated "Old Willow Fort". They uncovered the foundations of nine log buildings, with cellars containing broken crockery and bottles, lead bullets, gun parts and military buttons; remnants of a timber palisade were found to the east, and defensive earthworks on the crest of the escarpment.

Forty years later, a group of volunteers, the Fort Willow Improvement Group, began to restore the site as an interpretive centre. Now part of the Nottawasaga Valley Conservation Area, it is maintained by the Friends of Historic Fort Willow.

With its interpretive signage, opposite, its picnic areas and network of trails, Historic Fort Willow is interesting any time of year, but never more so than in late September, when history comes alive during the Nine Mile Portage Heritage Festival.

ANDREW MARSHALL

The *Lady Elgin*, Engine No. 1 of the Ontario, Simcoe and Huron Union Railroad .

Transforming Ontario

Belching smoke and cinders, Ontario's first railway train steamed north from Toronto towards Machell's Corners (now Aurora) on May 16, 1853. Within two years, the Ontario, Simcoe and Huron Railroad, called Oats, Straw and Hay by the locals, had curved west of Barrie to the new lakeport of Collingwood on Georgian Bay.

Below: Lambton Flour Mills; a pen and ink drawing from 1893, by W. J. Thompson.

Opposite: The Grand Trunk Railway dock was daily abuzz with arrivals and departures of trains, steamships and wagons.

FROM THERE, steamboats transported goods and passengers quickly and cheaply to and from Lake Michigan's boomtown, Chicago, a city built on the Midwestern route that Cavelier de La Salle had travelled, on foot and by canoe, nearly 200 years earlier.

The railroad, renamed the Northern, avoided Lake Simcoe and the Nottawasaga Valley, and siphoned so much business away from Yonge Street at Holland Landing that traffic on the toll road fell into the doldrums. Three years later, the Grand Trunk Railroad had an equally drastic impact on the Toronto Carrying Place. Bypassing the Humber River south of the milltown of Weston, it ran parallel to the portage, now dubbed Weston Road, for several miles before crossing the river and heading west at the Wadsworth Mill. In 1871, the Toronto, Grey, Bruce railroad built a line beside it. Marvel of modern technology that it was, the iron horse still had to be fed cords of firewood and its huge boiler refilled with water; there was freight and baggage to be loaded and unloaded, and crew and passengers to be cared for. These tasks were done at assigned stations and Weston was one of those stations.

High-speed train travel to the City of Toronto, only minutes away, brought the rural hamlet into the city's industrial and financial orbit. Weston thrived as neighbouring villages dwindled and disappeared. Cruikshank's Wagon Works, Coulter's Foundry and Machine Shop, Cousins' Livery, Mallaby's Implement and Carriage, Thomson's

Photographed in 1889, the remants of William Gamble's mill became a backdrop for pleasant afternoon outings.

Ideal Bakery and other family businesses expanded on the land between Weston Road, the railways and the Wadsworth Mill.

By the 1870s, Charles and William Wads-worth had outlasted, and outsmarted, most of their competitors: John Scarlett's mills had shut down; Thomas Fisher at Millwood, and William Gamble, owner of the old King's Mill, had gone bankrupt. Gamble's big stone mill, gutted by fire, was a romantic ruin. The Wadsworth Mill, too, had burned down, but the brothers rebuilt it and added a woollen mill. Since buying the mill from James Farr in 1828, they and their sons had invested in modern machinery, most recently a steam engine, weathered flash floods, crop failures and economic depression, and avoided ruinous debt. They built houses for their workmen, and paid them fair wages.

Weston was a "company town" until it was incorporated as a village in 1881, but it was full of hustling, prosperous entrepreneurs with a strong belief in God, progress and education. The Roman Catholic and Anglican churches opened schools; the Methodists built a public school, and sent their daughters to ladies' colleges in Hamilton and Whitby.

Politically, Weston was Reform (Liberal). It had taken armed rebellions in Upper and Lower Canada in 1837 to persuade Britain that Canada should be an independent, democratic nation; when the Dominion of Canada came into being in 1867, Weston's voters (though men only) could freely express their opinions, whatever the Wadsworths might think.

William Lyon Mackenzie

AT TWILIGHT on December 6, 1837, William Lyon Mackenzie, a hot-tempered Reform politician, newspaper publisher and, in 1834, the City of Toronto's first mayor, led an armed mob on a march down Yonge Street to overthrow the government of Upper Canada. The rebellion was a populist uprising against an arbitrary, abusive and self-serving colonial administration that had long treated citizens' grievances with contempt: Mackenzie himself had been beaten up by Tory thugs and repeatedly expelled from the Legislative Assembly.

Though a fearless agitator, Mackenzie was no general. His rebel army, undisciplined, confused, with many carrying only pitchforks and sharpened sticks, panicked and fled at the first volley of musket fire from loyalist militiamen. The next day, those who had not deserted were routed from their base at Montgomery's Tavern on Yonge Street north of Eglinton Road. Mackenzie and a companion escaped to the north on horseback, then, on foot, doubled back to the southwest, fed and sheltered by sympathizers on the rural roads. To avoid capture, and execution, Mackenzie was running for the United States.

"We made for the Humber Bridge, through Vaughan, but found it strongly guarded," he told his biographer, Charles Lindsey. "Went up the river a long way, got some supper at the house of a farmer, crossed the stream on a foot bridge and by two next morning reached the hospitable mansion of a worthy settler on Dundas Street utterly exhausted with cold and fatigue."

Mackenzie's story is vague, possibly to protect the identities of his friends, but he seems to have walked a portion of the old Toronto portage south to the Humber Bridge at Dundas Street, the main highway to the west, then north again to the footbridge. There were so few settlers in the area at the time it's tempting to think that the hospitable mansion belonged to wealthy miller William Cooper. Mackenzie crossed the American border safely a day or two later. In 1850, pardoned by a Reform government, he returned to Toronto and died there, a loyal and chastened Canadian, in 1861.

William Lyon Mackenzie, the first mayor of the City of Toronto

Toronto Harbour, at the foot of Church Street, c. 1850. The rapid growth of the city along the waterfront can be clearly seen. Opposite right: The Eagle House was a fixture of social and commercial life in Weston at the turn of the twentieth century.

APART FROM the Sons of Temperance, perhaps, life was not all toil and prayer. The community's hotspot was the Eagle House, a handsome, two-storey brick inn and tavern on Weston Road. The Eagle House served as a handy outlet for the products of the mill's distillery (the Wadsworths fed the mash to hogs and sold them, too) and a popular destination for Torontonians out for a Sunday jaunt. An attempt was made to pave Weston Road with planks, but they broke so badly that they were more of a hazard than the mud. Travel on horseback, or by buggy, bicycle, and later, car, was preferable to the hot, sooty railway carriages. Dances were held in a spacious room over the inn's carriage shed; the dance floor had raised, rounded corners for Saturday roller skating.

By 1907, which was Weston Public School's fiftieth anniversary, the village could boast about its public library, electric light plant, streetcar service to Toronto, Bank of British North America, the foundry and works of the Moffat Stove Company, a newspaper and printing shop, a drugstore, grocers, dairies and greenhouses, including A. M. Barton's Chrysanthemum House. Several brick mansions outshone the Wadsworths' Pine Hills estate.

To the south, a young Toronto developer, Robert Home Smith, was transforming the Humber River Valley into an equally progressive, but strikingly different "Garden City". On behalf of English financiers, Home Smith bought up

COURTESY OF THE WESTON HISTORICAL SOCIETY

Ontario zoologist and artist Edmund Murton Walker's "Suffolk sheep grazing on the savannah" aptly illustrates developer Robert Home Smith's catch-phrase, "a little bit of England, far from England".

3,000 acres of farm and valley land, including James Baby's country estate, Jean-Baptiste Rousseaux's old homestead, and the burned-out King's Mill. Home Smith subdivided his property into "parks", spacious treed lots fronting streets that followed the contours of the land. Buyers might hire their own architects, but they had to conform to a code: "Builders must build in stone and roughcast or stucco and must live in the Park." Apart from doctors and dentists seeing patients in their home offices, no retail or commercial development was allowed; garages for cars were accommodated, stables were not. Park space featured tennis courts and lawn bowling greens.

Advertising his suburban havens as "a little bit of England, far from England", Home Smith opened a restaurant and tea room in the Old Mill on August 4, 1914, the day England and Canada went to war with Germany for five anguished years. Not to worry; after the war, the prestige and exclusivity of Baby Point and the South Kingsway attracted young families enriched by the discovery of gold and silver in northern Ontario, or by their own brilliant opportunism.

One of them, at 68 Baby Point Road, was a smart, scrappy, hockey promoter, Conn Smythe. Famous as the founder of the Toronto Maple Leafs hockey team in 1927, Smythe made his first fortune in the sand and gravel business. In 1920, just out of the army, he bought a few acres of land east of the Humber River north of Black

Canoeing on the Humber River was a favourite pursuit. Here, developer Robert Home Smith's family and friends enjoy an outing about 1895. The Old Mill (or King's Mill, as it was once known) where the developer would one day open a restaurant and tea room, can be seen in the background.

Discovered in 2006 by Toronto's Archaeological Services at the site of Teiaiagon, this delicate comb, carved from a moose antler, has been dated to the 1680s. It is believed to have been worn by a Seneca woman.

Creek that had once been a sandbar in glacial Lake Iroquois. Starting out with a five-ton truck painted blue with white lettering, "C. Smythe for Sand", Smythe cashed in on road construction and concrete. Maple Leaf Gardens endures today as a monument to both his talents.

UNLIKE SMYTHE, who had no reason to suspect he might be destroying ancient campsites occupied by Ontario's First Peoples, Robert Home Smith ignored archaeological evidence that Baby Point was the site of the seventeenth-century Iroquois village, Teiaiagon. In the 1880s, James Baby's son Raymond, who lived on the property, had pointed out to archaeologist David Boyle a burial ground and a campground or village site where relics had been turned up by the plough. "A number of native burial pits have been opened at various times," Boyle reported, "and much valuable material taken from them. It is quite certain that when this portion of the farm is freed from underbrush further interesting discoveries will be made." The site had already been scavenged by "an enthusiastic collector", James Kirkwood, who donated to Boyle's museum two ground stone gouges, about 7,000 years old, a ceramic pipe and a birdstone. There is no catalogue of any other artifacts, which Raymond Baby may have kept, and the property, though often visited by amateur archaeologists, was not systematically examined.

Wild animal bones and iron tomahawks were discovered in the 1920s by Baby Point's new home-owners exploring the wooded slope leading down to the river, but the first professional investigation was made as the result of a mishap in 1999. A backhoe digging a trench for a gas line uncovered a human burial, a woman in her twenties, stretched out in a shallow pit, her head to the west and her left arm crossed over her chest. Her right arm and portions of her right torso had been destroyed by the backhoe.

The skeleton wore two brass rings on her left hand; on her right side were the remnants of a brass kettle containing a scrap of fur. Another brass finger ring and a carved antler comb depicting two human figures wearing European-style clothes were recovered from the disturbed soil.

The artifacts indicated that a Seneca woman had died at Teiaiagon between 1650 and 1675. In July 2006, Toronto's Archaeological Services Inc. examined a grave of a second, much older woman, on South Baby Point Crescent. A knife, an iron axe and a brass pot containing an ash bowl with remnants of squash, acorn and grapes, indicated European contact during the same period, but this woman had been buried with an engraved antler comb of exceptional power and artistry. The engraving shows a recumbant Seneca panther effigy that appears to morph into a bear embracing a human figure on the panther's back. Bears are sacred in many Aboriginal cultures, including the Algonquian-speaking people of the Great Lakes and the sinuous creatue may represent Mi-shi-pi-zhiw, the Algonquin's Great Underwater Wildcat.

The modern Humber River; the Carrying Place followed the ridge shown at the bottom of this photograph, along the east side of the river.

Rollicking Humber Bay

WINDY HUMBER BAY, shunned as a harbour in the age of sail, escaped the industrialization that buried Toronto's waterfront under brick, stone and concrete in the age of steam. Isolated from the downtown by 400-acre High Park, Sunnyside Beach and Amusement Park, as well as the Canadian National Exhibition Grounds, the bay developed into a summer playground easily reached by boat, or, after 1893, the Toronto and Mimico Electric Railway. Spawning salmon, once speared by torchlight at the river's mouth, virtually disappeared after mill dams barred their way upriver, but a patient fisherman might catch a fine trout or whitefish, and for birdwatchers, the Humber marshes were a sanctuary. Marinas rented out canoes for leisurely paddles upstream to secluded bays or tea rooms, and sponsored rowing regattas for muscular young Argonauts. After 1903, wealthy Toronto sportsmen could take a Saturday CPR train to the new Lambton Golf Club on the Humber flats, where William Cooper and John Scarlett had once sawn trees, ground wheat into flour, and made whiskey.

Drinking, dining and dancing were Humber Bay's great attractions. Toronto the Good, a city proud of its churches, was painfully puritan on weekends, but Humber Bay, outside the city's boundaries, was jumping. Old Mother McLean's tavern was soon eclipsed by marinas, hotels and restaurants with banquet halls and dance floors. While some, such as the Royal Oak Hotel, built around an ancient oak tree, were classy, others were rowdy. An ox roast on John Duck's picnic grounds in the 1880s turned into a brawl when a mob of revellers arrived with kegs of beer. Duck's grounds featured a menagerie of wild animals, including a bear, and at the height of the donnybrook a man was tossed into the bear's cage. He was rescued unharmed by a policeman who had seen the incident from his safe perch in a tree.

John Duck's Hotel and picnic grounds on Humber Bay, shown here in 1878, attracted revellers by rail, road and sail. This drawing first appeared in the Illustrated Historical Atlas *of the county of York.*

J. Duck's Hotel and Pleasure Grounds, Humber-Mouth.

Above: The Humber Bay Regatta in 1922. Right: The Humber River looking north from The Queensway the same year.
Both photographs first appeared in The Globe.

AS THE SOUTHERN Carrying Place became urban and suburban, the great marsh on the West Holland River to the north was drained for market gardens. The "quagmire" that had bogged down Governor Simcoe's expedition in 1793 had been an earthly paradise for the Ojibwe chief Great Sail, but in a later era when agriculture was regarded as the economic and moral backbone of the nation, fish, deer and ducks were of value only to sportsmen, and beaver a nuisance. By the 1880s, however, settlers near the village of Bradford were harvesting marsh hay and selling it in Toronto as packing and mattress stuffing. If the meadows could be profitable, why not reclaim the rest of the swamp?

In 1852, it had been proposed to lower the water level of Lake Simcoe, and drain the marsh, by deepening the outlet from Lake Couchiching to the Severn River; with more water from both lakes rushing north to Georgian Bay, acres of swamp and lake bottom would become dry land. Nothing came of this scheme, or of a plan to transform the Humber, Holland and Nottawasaga Rivers into a canal, but in 1910, William Day, a physics professor at the Ontario College of Agriculture in Guelph, proposed draining the marsh by dredging canals. Day was so enthusiastic about the thick black muck's potential for growing vegetables that he formed a syndicate with Bradford area investors to buy 4,000 acres of marshland and finance the canal's construction, yet fifteen years passed before the Holland Marsh Drainage

The "earth-devouring monster" that dredged the Marsh's original canals.

Scheme – called The Big Scheme – was hesitantly approved by the townships and landowners involved.

On August 10, 1925, the *Newmarket Era* reported:

There now lies in the stocks on the southern bank of the Holland River, beside the Barrie Highway leading to Toronto, a scow staunchly built of British Columbia fir. It is 80 feet long, 30 feet wide and has a depth of seven feet. Across its decks are big timbers that are to carry the amphibian monster, which will stick its nose down into the muck and clay, and while it builds a dyke likewise will cut its seventeen-mile circuit around the flats.

THE JONKMAN COLLECTION / COURTESY OF THE TOWNSHIPS OF KING AND BRADFORD WEST GWILLIMBURY

As it cuts its way it will drag itself along through the mud and slime. The 65-foot boom of steel sticks in front drooping a dipper with a sixty-foot handle. It will take a two-cubic-yard mouthful every time it goes down and it has a downward reach of 30 feet. The progress of this earth-devouring monster will depend on the type of soil it has to dig. On the top is a dressing of muck that will be literally 'pie' for it, but underneath there is a bed of clay that will require plenty of steam to rip it up.

Wallowing west from Bradford, the dredge dug a canal seven feet deep that narrowed from seventy feet wide at the top to thirty-eight feet. Over the next four years, a network of canals, dams and pumping stations began to channel water out of the marsh. The first farmer was William Day. In 1930, Day, who had moved his family to a thirty-seven-acre muck farm near Bradford, happily reported that he had sold his last year's crop of lettuce, celery, onions, carrots and parsnips for $26,000. Day did not trumpet the costs of seed, fertilizer, planting, harvesting, crating and trucking that ate up half his profits, or the debt, taxes and operating costs the syndicate had to pay on its expensive investment. The Great Depression would bankrupt the syndicate and the Dutch would reclaim Samuel Holland's marsh.

An accident brought Dutch settlers to this Canadian swamp, which had been named in 1793 for their kinsman, surveyor Samuel Holland. In the summer of 1931, a young Dutch immigrant, John Sytema, was driving through Bradford on his way north to Algonquin Park when his car broke down. As he waited for it to be repaired, he noticed William Day's lush vegetable garden near the road. Sytema's only experience with agriculture came from his work as a farmhand in the Dutch community near Hamilton, but he wanted to buy land, and he listened eagerly as Day sang the marsh's praises. Three years earlier, convinced that the Dutch were the world's best marsh farmers, Day had brought three families from the Netherlands to work on his land; in 1929, another Dutch family, the Rols, had become tenant farmers for Bradford landowner A.J. Saint. Sytema wanted more than a summer job that paid $2.50 for a ten-hour day.

Tilling the soil was an enormous task for many years, though here the toil is broken as two workers ham it up for the camera.

Within days, Sytema and two partners, Henry Poelman and Peter Greyn, had purchased 175 acres of unworked land for $35 an acre, with payments to start after the third year. Sytema and Greyn cleared the tangled underbrush and ploughed enough wet, black soil to plant a few rows of lettuce and carrots the following spring. They spent the summer of 1932 pulling weeds. It was hot, dirty, backbreaking toil, but unlike most marsh pioneers, they didn't give up. At a time when jobs of any kind were scarce, and unemployed immigrants faced deportation, they were at least landowners working for themselves.

As the Holland Marsh, drained and cultivated, began to bear a striking resemblance to the Netherlands' own flat, treeless, diked lands, or polders, John Snor, a Dutch antique dealer in Hamilton who acted as agent for the Netherlands Emigration Foundation, seized his opportunity to create a Dutch colony in the marsh. A 125-acre parcel of undeveloped land in King Township was subdivided into twenty-five five-acre lots. Each settler received a $600 grubstake, $200 apiece from the federal, provincial and Dutch governments, to build a house, buy seed and tools and pay their living expenses until they be-

A row of nearly identical gambrel-roofed houses line the road in Ansnorveldt.

came self-supporting. The $500 cost of their plot of land could be repaid over time.

By the summer of 1934, Snor had recruited seventeen Dutch families from the Hamilton area, most of them members of the same Christian Reformed Church. The men and their older sons ploughed the land, digging out the gigantic roots of ancient trees, and built almost identical two-storey frame houses, each sixteen by twenty feet, in a row fronting on the Concession 3 road allowance. The houses were raised on cedar poles, three feet above ground level, in case of flooding. Clean water had to be hauled in pails from a communal artesian well, and the whole house was heated by the woodstove in the kitchen. The little hamlet was named Ansnorveldt, "On Snor's Field", in honour of its founder.

Planting the first crops was guesswork. No one, Snor included, really knew what would grow best in this part of the marsh. "To the naked eye, the black muck at Ansnorveldt looked extremely rich and capable of supporting any crop," Albert VanderMey writes in *And the Swamp Flourished.* "That's why, at first, it was highly prized. Experience determined that a great deal of chemical fertilizer had to be applied to the soil in the spring to supply a long list of lacking nutrients. Actually, all the muck did was support the roots and hold moisture for the plant. And then there were the dust storms, especially during dry periods. The wind lifted the arid soil and sent it through the air in a suffocating cloud. It drifted like snow, banking up around buildings and filling in the drainage ditches."

During planting and harvesting, the whole family laboured in the fields from sunrise to sunset. Thinning and weeding the rows by hand, often on their knees, was the summer's hot, tedious work. Marketing the vegetables was a challenge when the bags and crates of potatoes, carrots, onions and lettuce, cleaned and sorted, had to be trucked long distances to towns and cities, customers were frugal, produce spoiled quickly and most farmers, too poor to buy their own trucks, had to rely on wholesalers from Toronto. At least the Dutch could eat their own produce. Single men and some families spent the winters working in towns and cities when Ansnorveldt became a lonely speck on a snowy, windswept plain.

"In a way, all immigrants are pioneers," says VanderMey.

They say goodbye to what is dear and familiar and strike out resolutely for alien shores, intending to delve into the unknown and emerge somehow in a better world. The cluster of Marsh people, however, had gone a step further; while still adjusting themselves to a different culture, language, climate and geography, they had decided to move to an area where, figuratively, no one had been before and launch a new existence from scratch.

People so bold must possess certain qualities: an imagination to see a future few others can perceive, *perseverance to pull them through unthinkable situations, a willingness to get by with only the bare necessities, an ingenuity to work wonders with next to nothing, lots of optimism, and faith in themselves and in God.*

Sunday was a day of rest, and sermons, read in Dutch by Ansnorveldt elders in one of their houses, were so popular that a small, frame Christian Reformed Church was built in the spring of 1935. A one-room public school followed in September. Stores in Bradford delivered milk daily, groceries weekly, all on credit until the autumn harvest. It was a virtuous community; the church forbade going to moves, dances or beer parlours, although young rebels could hitchhike into Newmarket for a Saturday night on the town.

In good weather, John Snor and his wife Cornelia drove down Ansnorveldt's dirt road, stopping to ask the homesteaders how they were doing. "Getting by, just barely," was the usual curt reply. Poor as they were, they were better off than on relief, but Snor, described as "proud" and "ruthless", was growing rich selling marsh properties to immigrants.

The Marsh people had come to stay, and over the years their numbers grew. World War II, which caused great suffering in Nazi-occupied Holland, brought prosperity to the Holland Marsh. With thousands of young Canadian men and women in uniform to be fed, and a widespread scarcity

While automation helped lessen some of the backbreaking work endured by the Marsh people, hard labour was still required for many decades. Here, workers pick lettuce by hand in the 1950s.

of agricultural products, the market gardeners were able to sell everything they harvested. After the war, when shiploads of European and Ukrainian immigrants provided cheap labour on farms across Canada, the Netherlands-Canadian Settlement Scheme encouraged farmers to sponsor families. In exchange for free housing, and a minimum monthly wage of $75 for a married man, the family agreed to stay for at least a year; children, when not in school, were assumed to be part of the labour force. Going to school usually meant a walk of four or five miles along dirt roads that were sometimes impassable in winter. Most homes had party-line telephones, but no electricity – families sat around the glow of kerosene lamps when the day's work was done, and toilets were usually outdoors.

Modern technology soon transformed vegetable growing from hardscrabble home gardening into a profitable industry. Refrigeration allowed potatoes and carrots to be stored in warehouses and marketed into the winter; "farm fresh" lettuce and celery were shipped long distances in ice cold railway cars. Marsh produce began to appear in stores and restaurants in Detroit and New York City and across Canada. Produce once dumped because it was wilted or rotted was worth millions, and in Bradford, packing houses and cold storage plants created new jobs and business opportunities. By 1954, twenty years after the Dutch had built their first flimsy houses, Ansnorveldt had grown into an up-to-date, picturesque, yet still staunchly Calvinist community. Nobody called the Marsh people crazy anymore. They had tamed the wilderness. Or had they?

Opposite: A Dutch family on the SS Nieuw-Amsterdam, *en route to Canada in 1951.*

Below: after World War II, planting and harvesting many crops, including onions and carrots, was increasingly mechanized.

The Toronto

and

Georgian Bay Ship Canal

THE VISION of a ship canal connecting Lake Ontario to Lake Huron captured the imaginations of many Ontario businessmen in the mid-nineteenth century. Their goal was to permit steamships to travel from Europe to Chicago, possibly to Lake Superior, and the three routes promoted were the Ottawa River, the Trent and Severn Rivers, and the Humber-Holland-Nottawasaga Rivers. The passionate proponent of the third, Carrying Place route was a man who had made his fortune on it, Rowland Burr. In 1837, Burr, a carpenter by trade, built a flour mill at the junction of the Humber and East Humber Rivers, a short distance west of the vanished Huron villages, and laid out lots for his own village, which he named Burwick. He soon added a saw mill and woolen mill, but no distillery; a Quaker turned Methodist, Burr refused to compromise his prohibitionist convictions. By 1851, Burr had sold his profitable mills in the village now known as Woodbridge, and retired to Toronto to preach Reform, temperance and his Toronto and Georgian Bay Ship Canal.

With Ontario's Rideau and Welland Canals proven successes, and the world agog about the proposed Suez Canal linking the Mediterranean Ocean and the Red Sea, Burr's idea did not seem preposterous. Burr had inspected the route himself, and the Toronto Board of Trade had hired an engineer to confirm that an eighty-mile canal was possible. It would be twelve feet deep and 120 feet wide, with sixty-four locks of cut stone; the cost was estimated at between twenty and thirty million dollars.

The most serious, if not impossible, challenge was to dig a deep, wide ditch through the Oak Ridges Moraine to connect the East Humber to the West Holland River, and another along the Nine Mile Portage between Kempenfelt Bay and the Nottawasaga River. In that era, the environmental impact of such a gargantuan reconstruction of the landscape was not investigated, though it may have subtly contributed to the project's failure.

By 1857, Burr had managed to interest some Canadian and American investors, but they wanted millions of acres of free land as payment, and Canadian politicians, hesitant to choose one costly canal over another, ignored them all. Most significantly, the Ontario, Simcoe and Huron Railway had reached Georgian Bay from Toronto in 1855; the smart money was on trains.

Rowland Burr may have been inspired by images, like this one, of the Rideau Canal. It was described by its creator, Captain Thomas Burrowes, as "Lower Bytown, from the Barrack Hill (later Parliament Hill), near the head of the Eighth Lock and the Sappers' Bridge". Burrowes had served as a surveyor and overseer during the canal's construction.

Chaos reigned in Holland Marsh on Saturday, October 16, 1954, the day after Hurricane Hazel hit.

Hurricane Hazel

and the Holland Marsh

October 15, 1954:

"That Friday began as each previous day, with rain, except this fell steadily heavier until it became a cloudburst. The weeks before had been wet ones, and the fields had already reached the saturation point. However, the sky did clear for about half an hour around 11 a.m. I believe this was the beginning of the hurricane." – Addy Radder Ellens

Storm Brings Death, Delay And Darkness

Twenty-four hours battering by rain and gale-force winds left a huge slice of Southwestern Ontario in a state of havoc last night, and hour by hour the picture of damage and destruction grew grimmer.

Even before the midnight deadline set for Hurricane Hazel's onslaught, millions of

ADDY RADDER lived with her parents, Nellie and Cornelius, in the hamlet of Springdale at the northwestern tip of the Holland Marsh. For days they had been anxiously watching the water level rise in the canal, worrying whether the dike would hold. The news on the radio was ominous. Hurricane Hazel was whirling north from the Caribbean, heading directly for Toronto. Hazel had devastated the island of Haiti, killing more than 1,000 people, and, unlike other hurricanes, she had not blown herself out over the Atlantic Ocean. By the time Marsh families began to drive out to higher ground on Friday evening, flood water was rushing across the low-lying roads and bridges, and a landslide had blocked part of Highway 400. Was it safer to stay? The Dominion weather office, downgrading Hazel to an "extratropical cyclone", forecast only "occasional light rain throughout the night" as the weakening storm passed east of Toronto.

Addy remembers: "By supper time, word spread that the dikes would not be able to hold back the rush of water pouring in from the highland. Men and boys filled sandbags to raise the dike. This was soon seen as useless and most thought the water would come over the dike, but would not exceed the main floor of their homes. Our grocery store was in the middle of the Marsh, similar to the middle of a saucer. We began to move groceries from the lower to higher shelves. Then we left the store and my boyfriend Auke attempted to drive his truck to the canal dike, as most others had done. It kept stalling and he finally left it and walked to my parents' home down the road from the store. My Dad had opened the trap door in the floor of the house to allow the water to come in so it wouldn't float away. Then we (my mother and father and brother Leon and Auke) went upstairs to wait out the storm.

"Around 11 p.m., the rain slowed down and the wind stilled. Dad called us out to the front porch. The water was all around us and we could hear it falling over the dike. 'You are standing in the eye of the storm,' he said. 'Soon the wind will rise from the opposite direction and the rain will fall as heavily as before.' He was so right. After that brief respite, the storm returned as savage as before. Before the water reached the telephone downstairs in the front hall, we tried to call a neighbour who lived along the dike to hear how things were, knowing the worst news would be better than not knowing anything. We could not get through. The telephone was no longer working.

"Then began a long night of howling winds and driving rain. In 1953, a storm on the North Sea had devastated Zeeland and the surroundings areas in The Netherlands. More than 1,000 people lost their lives. I knew that people had tied themselves to chimneys to escape the rising water. I wondered if we could survive if the water chased us out onto the roof. We watched at the windows and soon saw a strange sight. There came, as if it were a ghost ship, a house approaching,

Above: Flooded King Street in the Holland Marsh; below, a raised farmyard became an island.

BOTH PHOTOS: THE JONKMAN COLLECTION / COURTESY OF THE TOWNSHIP OF KING AND BRADFORD GWILLIMBURY

A midnight escape by boat

riding the waves. It was clearly visible because it was so near and white. It hit the barn and then swerved and crashed into the greenhouse, caught on something and whirled around and passed our house and caught in the hydro wires where it stopped. We did not know at the time if the family was in the house or not."

The Radders and Auke Ellens were rescued in the morning by men in boats from Bradford; a flat part of their roof served as a dock. The ghost house proved to have been empty, and the family safe, but the storm had sent the nearby de Peuter family on a harrowing journey. Survivors of the deadly floods in the Netherlands, the de Peuters – John, his wife and twelve children, along with a visitor, had been living in the Holland Marsh barely six months when Hazel struck. As they waited to be rescued, water began pouring into their house. John nailed the doors shut, plugged the cracks and hustled the children, including a neighbour's son, upstairs. Suddenly, there was a terrific jolt: a surge of water from the breached dike had lifted the house off its pilings and set it adrift amid a shower of sparks from ripped hydro wires.

"The house just took off like a boat, a real Noah's Ark," fifteen-year-old Harry de Peuter tells Betty Kennedy in her book, *Hurricane Hazel.* "From 11:30 till 6:30 we floated aimlessly through the Marsh, bumping into houses, greenhouses, barns, hydro poles, everything. The area over by the Holland River had a faster current

THE JONKMAN COLLECTION / COURTESY OF THE TOWNSHIPS
OF KING AND BRADFORD GWILLIMBURY

The de Peuter house, once again "docked" on land, the day after its violent ride through the marsh. Remarkably all fifteen occupants of the house survived.

and somehow our house got caught in that current and started spinning like a top, faster and faster, rocking to and fro. We all – all fifteen of us – would run from one side of the house to the other when it tilted, trying to balance it out. One of my younger brothers, Bastian, got violently seasick.

"Until then, we had been too busy to really worry and then one of the younger ones asked if we were all going to die. My mother said that only one person knew that, the Lord, and we all knelt down and prayed, the Lord's Prayer. And we did get out of the current and finally came to rest against a service road near the 400, where a complete field of carrots had floated up to the surface and helped hold us in place."

The de Peuters waved bedsheets from the windows to attract the attention of motorists on the highway. An amphibious army truck drove close enough for a diver to attach a rope to the house; clinging to the rope, a man in a tippy canoe evacuated the family, two by two.

One Holland Marsh man, John Nagy, was drowned in Hurricane Hazel. In Greater Toronto, south of the Oak Ridges Moraine, the rainstorm took eighty-one lives that dark night, many of them young families living on the Humber River's flood plains in Woodbridge and Weston. A flash flood in 1850 had wiped out the original settlement of Weston on the river's west bank, but that was long ago, and the flats were attractive locations for house builders. The lazy, winding river deceived them. To the north, more than a century of clear-cut logging had stripped the moraine's dry clay hills of the topsoil and vegetation that absorbed rainwater; agriculture had silted up gullies and filled in wetlands. The crumbling dams and sluices of the Humber's many old, decayed mills clogged the river's watercourse. As Hazel's relentless rain pelted down, a wild, rebellious Humber River roared towards Lake Ontario.

By nightfall, water was running across major city roads and flooding underpasses. Cars stalled, their occupants clinging to their roofs as the water rose. Some motorists, blinded by the rain, drove into chasms where roads and bridges had been washed out. In Woodbridge, postmaster

Opposite: In the Woodbridge Trailer Park, the surging water threw the trailers around like tin cans, toppling them and dumping them on top of cars.

Cecil Rowe stood by a bridge that was a foot under water, warning drivers to turn back. One couple, with their seven-year-old daughter and family dog, refused. "They suddenly roared off to get across the bridge," Rowe told Betty Kennedy. "At the moment they hit the centre, a great flood-crest hit the bridge, tearing the railings down and sweeping the car and occupants away. We could see the headlights bobbing for the longest time and could only guess at the terror they felt. They were found drowned the next day."

Staying home, out of the rain and gusting winds, made sense to many; they crawled into bed, watched television, and waited for the morning. Leslie Phillips, playing cards with his brother-in-law in his riverbank trailer in the Woodbridge Trailer Park, became alarmed when he stepped outside into ankle-deep running water; by the time he'd put on his rubber boots, the water was up to his boot tops.

The two young men hastily woke Leslie's wife Dorothy and carried her to the car. Churning through the slick mud to high ground, they returned to rescue a family whose car was mired. A short time later, a surge of water scattered the park's fifty trailers, crushing them like tin cans.

As dams gave way and old bridges collapsed, the river's current gathered strength. Downstream from Weston, a swing bridge, partly torn from its moorings, channelled the torrent directly towards the modest frame and stucco homes on Raymore Drive. About midnight, Annie and Joe Ward

Hurricane Hazel and the Holland Marsh

were roused from sleep by water pouring across their living room floor. Then a huge tree crashed through the front window. The Wards scrambled up to the attic and clawed a hole in the roof barely big enough to climb through. Their house seemed to be listing. On the roof, they saw that it was shoved against a neighbour's; they jumped across as their chimney crumbled. Huddled against the cold wind, they watched flashlights winking in other houses as people tried to escape. Then the flashlights went out.

"The homes were literally lifted off their foundations and swept away," said eyewitness Dave Phillips. "You could hear the people screaming. Many of them were standing on their roofs. In many cases the screaming just stopped; the homes just disintegrated, and that was the end of it." Raymore Drive was obliterated in a little more than an hour. Annie and Joe Ward were among the sixty homeless families who survived; thirty-five people drowned, among them nine members of one family, including six children.

Police, firefighters, armed forces personnel and volunteers with boats rescued hundreds of people marooned on their roofs and porches. The rescuers put themselves in great danger. At the height of the storm, the Kingsway-Lambton Fire Department dispatched a pumper truck with a crew of eight to River Road, north of the Old Mill. People had been reported stranded on top of a car, but as driver James Britton inched the heavy fire truck down the swampy road, already under water, he saw the car was empty. Surrounded by mud, the road behind invisible, the firemen decided to park their truck, climb up on their stack of ladders and hoses, and radio their location.

As Britton later told Betty Kennedy: "You know, I grew up here. Oh, we've seen the Humber in flood. We used to go down, little bare-assed kids … to play off the islands. As we figured, OK, fine. But the water kept coming. Up to the tires. Getting higher. And higher. But you know, we know this river. We were getting concerned. But we weren't upset."

Police arrived, but the current capsized the little dinghy they tried to launch. Britton, a rope around his waist, tried to reach a chain link fence up the embankment, but his feet were swept out from under him. The fire truck, its engine running and lights blazing, began to roll over; the men shook hands, said goodbye and jumped into the river. Britton and two others survived.

The sun rose on two broad, turgid lakes that had not been there the day before. In some parts of the Holland Marsh the water was ten feet deep, and the last of the year's onion crop was floating on the surface; the Humber Valley was awash with uprooted trees and tangled wreckage. Half-submerged houses dotted the lakes like islands.

Survivors gazed on the devastation with sorrow, horror and awe. In the Marsh, farmers reacted with defiance. They had fought off the Holland River once, and won; they would fight again. As soon as the homeless were cared for, dikes were quickly repaired and the water pumped out. Some farmers believed that the flood improved the quality of the soil, and their farms were long overdue for a good clean-up.

On the Humber, where the first task was to retrieve the bodies of the dead, the mood was elegiac, remorseful, apologetic. For decades, scientists and conservationists had been raising alarms about the degradation of the watershed. In 1948, the first report of the Humber Valley Conservation Authority had warned that the river was polluted with sewage and industrial waste, and that soil erosion and deforestation made flooding a constant threat. As early as 1860, sawdust and waste from the mills and tanneries had, along with the dams, destroyed the river's salmon fishery; by 1900, the mills had gone out of business after all the trees has all been cut, and the upland creeks were clogged with silt washed down from the denuded hills.

Hurricane Hazel's voice was heard. No more housing developments or trailer parks would be built on the floodplain: Raymore Drive, "the street that never was", became a memorial park. In the years to come, a chain of parks, golf courses, sports fields and conservation areas would line both banks of the river from its swampy mouth to the wilderness area on the East Humber River between Woodbridge and Kleinburg, home to the Kortright Centre for Conservation and the

Opposite: Hurricane Hazel took less than a day to return Holland Marsh, so painstakingly drained and planted, to the wetland it had for been so many centuries.

McMichael Canadian Art Collection. To the north, thousands more acres of land have been protected and reforested, and property owners have been encouraged to plant native trees.

This ambitious, complex and expensive initiative, undertaken in 1957 by the Metropolitan Toronto Region Conservation Authority (MTRCA), now the Toronto Region Conservation Authority (TRCA), continues. Flood control was the first, most urgent priority, but in spite of a series of dams, reservoirs and channels upstream, the Humber frequently floods; in the spring of 2009, an ice jam north of the Old Mill swamped Étienne Brûlé park, and much of the floodplain is still occupied by residential and commercial development.

Mistakes were made. The lower reach of Black Creek was encased in a hideous concrete straightjacket, and a series of six solid concrete weirs, each five feet high, destroyed the historic rapids that had marked the beginning of the Carrying Place. The weirs, intended to slow the river's pace in flood conditions, prevent most lake fish from swimming upstream.

Pollution remains a problem. A sewage treatment plant at the river's mouth might be considered a conservation measure, except that sewage from Toronto's antiquated pipes escapes into storm sewers during heavy rainfall. The Humber's beaches, like most in the city, are unsafe for swimming. Nonetheless, during the 1970s, the MTRCA allowed mountains of landfill – demolished buildings, dirt, clay, asphalt, garbage and junk – to be dumped into Toronto Harbour. Two man-made spits were built at Humber Bay's western point, with scant consideration for the impact of these landfills on water quality and the integrity of the landscape. Toronto is a city of almost three million people. Runoff water from streets and expressways carries oil, dirt and chemicals. Most toxic is chloride, from the road salt that saturates city streets in the winter months; three major expressways cross the Humber River at its mouth.

The riverbanks are home to a new population of cliff dwellers in highrise apartments and condominiums; to the north, forests of pine and hardwoods have been replaced by dense plantations of brick houses, the soil trucked away or paved over. Green spaces are heavily used, even overused, by hikers, cyclists, and, often illegally, by dirt bikes, all-terrain vehicles and snowmobiles.

Yet Hazel's voice was heard. Decades of advocacy, education and protest by naturalists, scientists, conservationists and citizens' organizations such as Save the Oak Ridges Moraine (STORM) have heightened public and political awareness about the value and fragility of the watershed. The Oak Ridges Moraine Protection Act restricts development to existing towns and villages – still too invasive for many critics – and requires the preservation and enhancement of natural features. The TRCA emphasizes naturalization and the restoration of wildlife habitat, including corridors that allow white-tailed deer, coyotes, raccoons and the occasional opossum to range over larger territories. Wetlands, once loathed as breeding grounds for mosquitoes and miasmal vapours, are now cherished for their populations of salamanders, frogs, turtles, great blue herons and rare species of songbirds.

The wilderness is slowly creeping back in the Happy Valley Forest, a 1000-hectare swath of woodland that straddles the Toronto Carrying Place atop the moraine. When Lieutenant-Governor Simcoe crossed these hills and valleys in 1793, he would have passed through an old growth forest of oak and white pine, timber much prized by the British for building ships. Soon, the giant trees were felled. According to local legend, life in the nineteenth-century logging camps was so harsh, the bosses so cruel, that the lumbermen named it Happy Valley in a fit of black humour. Homesteaders who settled on the cleared land could not grow crops on the sandy, infertile soil, and in the twentieth century a new, young forest of maple, beech, red oak, hemlock and white ash began to reclaim their abandoned farms. Wealthy Toronto families, the Pellatts, Eatons and Mulocks among them, bought hundreds of acres of waste moraine land for country estates; others found quiet and seclusion in Happy Valley.

In 2001, the Nature Conservancy of Canada began assembling property in Happy Valley through gifts, easements and purchases to create "an old growth forest in the making". Dead, rotting trees are valued as cozy homes for wood ducks, owls, porcupines and squirrels as the noisy

hammering of pileated woodpeckers reduces the trees to sawdust. Apart from taking down hazardous trees, and removing invasive species such as garlic mustard, dog strangling vine and common buckthorn, landowners are encouraged to park the lawn tractor, junk the weed-whacker, and enjoy the rhythm of the seasons.

In dramatic contrast, the intensively cultivated gardens of the Holland Marsh lie lower on the watershed to the east. Known as Ontario's "salad bowl" and "the carrot capital of Canada", the Marsh produces about $30 million worth of vegetables, mostly carrots and onions, annually. The farms are still small – most are under 30 hectares or about seventy acres – and predominantly family-owned, and the population, once dominated by the Dutch, is now a typically Canadian mix that includes Chinese, Japanese and

Otters, seen resting on a log with a sun-bathing turtle in a photograph taken on the Oak Ridge Moraine, are a sign of the ecosystem's returning health.

seasonal workers from Mexico and the Caribbean. Life on a muck farm remains a struggle to make ends meet. Caught between chronic low prices for their produce and escalating costs of fuel, fertilizer, machinery and wages, farmers make an average profit of $318 per acre, an annual income of $22,260 for a seventy-acre farm. Most families have at least one member with an off-farm job.

The growers are growing older, and the peaty soil is disappearing beneath their feet. In the eighty years since the Marsh was drained, some areas have lost almost two metres of soil, the accumulation of thousands of years of decomposition. Improved farming practices have reduced the loss to about twenty-five centimetres a year, but the canals that drain the water erode the fields, and the West Holland River, rejuvenated by conservation efforts in the Happy Valley Forest upstream, is strong, healthy and teeming with fish. The canals, widened and deepened after Hurricane Hazel, are dangerously close to the narrow roads on top of the old dikes; since 1954, eighteen people have drowned. A $25-million drainage project is underway to improve and relocate nearly twenty-eight kilometres of the canals, but until this work is completed in

2017, the Marsh might once again be inundated by a monster storm.

Will that be The Flood that restores the swamp to its boggy, unkempt self? Optimists give the Marsh farms another 200 years of productivity, pessimists, just fifty years; some old timers are surprised that the soil has lasted this long. In late summer, the brown, almost stagnant, canals are verdant aquatic gardens of grasses, sedges, cattails and shiny green slime. The swamp is channelled, but thriving. Might there be a bigger market for fish, frogs, waterfowl and greenspace than for carrots and onions? Would this justify relocating hundreds of people, and turning six-lane Highway 400 into a raised causeway?

Highway 400 is the current incarnation of the Toronto Carrying Place, and travel on it can be as slow, frustrating and hazardous as it was for La Salle on foot more than 300 years ago. The Carrying Place is a testament to human curiosity, endurance and ingenuity; the Wendat/ Huron made a "taronto," a clever structure of sticks, to trap fish at the mouths of the rivers. Like the First People, we, the Present People, live in a manufactured landscape.

BARRY WALLACE

Opposite: Today, Holland Marsh is known as "the carrot capital of Canada".

Right: Street signs in Holland Marsh recall the dramatic events of the past.

HURRICANE HAZEL AND THE HOLLAND MARSH

Epilogue

WALKING THE entire Toronto Carrying Place remains a dream for many people, but so much of the path has been lost that its exact location is uncertain – and there may well have been several trails at different times over its long history.

Ken Carter's digital maps, based on his study of numerous surveyors' maps, the hand-drawn map in Percy Robinson's *Toronto During the French Régime*, and his own hard foot-slogging, are the latest and best attempts to pinpoint the route. In the 1970s and 1980s, the King Township, Weston and Vaughan Historical Societies erected a few carved wooden signposts and cairns beside roads that the trail had crossed or paralleled, but these locations were determined by their visibility, the availability of land, and the lack of a recent, accurate survey. In 1994, archaeologist Dr. Shaun J. Austin tried to spy out the path from city streets and county roads, following the chain of aboriginal campsites and ossuaries from Toronto to Woodbridge, and then taking his cue from the lines of hydro towers that marched north along the height of land. North of Woodbridge, Austin found two recent cairns with maps showing that the Carrying Place branched west near the present village of Kleinburg, rejoining the main route at the foot of the moraine, however neither route has been scientifically verified.

The Toronto Region Conservation Authority would love to reopen the Toronto Carrying Place trail from Woodbridge to the Holland River, but most of the land – farms, woodlots, subdivisions, country estates – is privately owned, expensive and inaccessible. In the summer of 1976, a group of twenty-three high school students and teachers from Illinois set out from Montreal to recreate Cavalier de La Salle's 1681–1682 canoe journey to the mouth of the Mississippi River. Dressed in handmade, seventeeth-century voyageur clothing, their hair long and unkempt, they paddled painted fibreglass "birchbark" canoes laden with the leather baggage trunks La Salle would have used, carried muskets and sang voyageur songs while they studied the landscape and history of the voyage. From September 10 to 22, they portaged the urbanized Toronto Carrying Place from Lake Ontario to the Holland River, sleeping out under their canoes and relying for their food on dried peas, corn meal and the generosity of the Canadian "natives". Crossing Lake Huron and Lake Michigan to Chicago, the La Salle Expedition II arrived in New Orleans on April 15, 1977.

Will expeditions like this happen again, on the real path?

Following prodigious library and "foot-slogging" research, Ken Carter has superimposed what he believes to be the path of the Toronto Carrying Place on a modern digital map.

Notes & Sources

Introduction

Photographs and information about Le Sentier Partagé/The Shared Path, in French and English, are on the Société d'histoire de Toronto's website, www.sht.ca. The plaque has since been moved to a site south of the gas station. "Rousseaux" seems a misspelling, but Jean-Baptiste preferred it.

"Locating the Rousseaux Home-Site," by William J. Daniels, B.Sc.F, O.L.S. was published by The Rousseau Project/Le Project Rousseau in 1991.

Toronto During the French Régime, 1615–1793, by Percy J. Robinson, was originally published by Ryerson Press, Toronto, in 1933, and republished, with additions, by the University of Toronto in 1965. *A Diary of Mrs. John Graves Simcoe*, with a biography by newspaperman John Ross Robertson, was published by William Briggs in Toronto in 1911. It contains 237 illustrations, including 90 of Elizabeth Simcoe's sketches and paintings. Yonge Street was named for Sir George Yonge, Britain's secretary of war.

My authority for *Taranto* or *Toronto* as "trees or poles in water", is Humber College professor John Steckley, an expert on Wendat/Huron language and culture. An eighteenth-century French missionary, Father Pierre Potier, offered: "a tree in the water that serves as a bridge for crossing a river". See: *Special Places*, ed. Donald Chant, UBC Press, p.73. This interpretation is his alone. "Toronto" seems to be a misspelling.

Since 1995, the Fort Willow site has been preserved and interpreted by the Fort Willow Improvement Group, now the Friends of Historic Fort Willow, under the auspices of the Nottawasaga Valley Conservation Authority: www.nvca.on.ca. The actors were recruited by David Brunelle, the 9MP Festival's Living History Coordinator.

I: Building Southern Ontario

BOOKS:
Ontario Rocks: Three Billion Years of Environmental Change, by Nick Eyles, University of Toronto, Fitzhenry & Whiteside, Toronto, 2002, 339 pp. Colour maps, photos and illustrations.

The Physiography of Southern Ontario, by L.J. Chapman and D.J. Putnam, University of Toronto Press, 1973, 386 pp. 2nd edition.

ARTICLES:
"Illinoian to Late Wisconsinian Stratigraphy at Woodbridge, Ontario," by P.J. Karrow, J.H. McAndrews, B.B. Miller, A.V. Morgan, K.L. Seymour, O.L. White; *Canadian Journal of Earth Sciences*, Vol. 38 (2001), pp. 921-942. Available online.

II: Early People

BOOKS:
Journey to the Ice Age: Discovering an Ancient World, Peter L. Storck, UBC Press, 2004, 356 pp. As much autobiography and detective story as a scholarly study, Storck's book reveals as much about the practice of archaeology as it does about Ontario's Early Peoples.

The Archaeology of Southern Ontario, Christopher John Ellis, London Chapter, Ontario Archaeological Society, 1990. 570 pp.

Toronto: A Short Illustrated History of its First 12,000 Years, ed. Ronald F. Williamson, James Lorimer & Co., Toronto, 2008.

ARTICLES:
"A Multispecies Overkill Simulation of the End-Pleistocene Megafaunal Mass Extinction," John Alroy, *Science*, Vol. 292, pp. 1893-1896. "The simulation results are unambiguous," Alroy writes. "Human population growth and hunting almost invariably leads to a major mass extinction." Some scientists speculate that rather than being caused by climate change, the disappearance of millions of methane-producing herbivores caused the North American climate to cool.

"Glacial Lake Levels and Eastern Great Lakes Palaeo-Indians," Lawrence Jackson, Christopher Ellis, Alan V. Morgan, John H. McAndrews, *Geoarchaeology*, Vol. 15, No. 5, 415-440, 2000.

"Southeast Collector Recreational Enhancements East Branch of the Toronto Carrying Place: An Historical Overview," Archaeological Services Inc., 2009. Ron Williamson's quote comes from this report prepared by his company.

"The Boyd Site," W. S. Donaldson, *Ontario Archaeology*, 1962. Rowland Orr's quote comes from Ontario Archaeological Report, 21st-23rd, 1908-1911, Royal Ontario Museum. Norman Emerson briefly describes his work in this region in his unpublished memoir,

"Twenty-Five Years of Archaeology," University of Toronto Archives.

TORONTO REGION CONSERVATION AUTHORITY REPORTS: "Seed-Barker Site (AkGv-1)," 2009. Robert Burgar directed the Boyd Archaeological Field School from 1983 until 2005.

Draft "Humber River Watershed Cultural Heritage Study Background Report," 1996.

"Legacy: A Strategy for a Healthy Humber," Report of the Humber Watershed Task Force, 1997.

III: THE FRENCH

The Dictionary of Canadian Biography, (DCB) University of Toronto Press, is a comprehensive and reliable, but not infallible, source, 1000 to 1930. Free online.

Ontario's History in Maps, Louis Gentilcore, U of Toronto Press, 1984, 284 pp.

Historical Atlas of Toronto, Derek Hayes, Douglas & McIntyre, 2008, 192 pp.

The Beginnings of New France, 1524–1663, by Marcel Trudel, McClelland & Stewart, Toronto, 1973, 323 pp.

Étienne Brûlé's dramatic story has inspired several popular novels: *Le Sauvage Blanc*, by François D'Allaire; *Le Roman de Etienne Brulé*, by Michel Michaud; *No Man's Brother*, by Charles Ewart. A sympathetic biography was published in 1898: *History of Brulé's Discoveries and Explorations, 1610–1626*, Consul Willshire Butterfield, Helman-Taylor Company, Cleveland, Ohio. Butterfield gives Brûlé credit for his wide-ranging explorations, but anglicizes his name to Stephen. A lurid Canadian biography, *Étienne Brûlé: Immortal Scoundrel*, by J. Herbert Cranston, Ryerson, Toronto, was published in 1949. Novelists and biographers have relied on the same three principal sources: *The Works of Samuel de Champlain*, ed. H.P. Biggar, Toronto, Champlain Society, 1922-1936. *The Long Journey to the Country of the Huron*, by Father Gabriel Sagard, introduction and notes by George H. Wrong, translated by H.H. Langton, Champlain Society, 1939. It was originally published in French, with Sagard's Huron dictionary, in Paris, in 1865. A new edition, *Gabriel Sagard's Dictionary of Huron*, translated into English by John Steckley, was published in 2010 by ARL Supplement Series, Vol. 2, Evolution Publishing, Merchantville, NJ. The Jesuit Relations and Allied Documents, ed. R.G. Thwaites, Cleveland, Burrows, 1896. Free online at canadiana.org/eco. Most

relevant to this story are volumes 3, 5, 8, 10, 23, 29. Historians have tended to take these personal journals as objective, factual documents, without accounting for their religious, political and private agendas. That Brûlé traded with the English and ate meat on Fridays were major sins; otherwise, the details of his licentiousness and debauchery are unspecified. The Wendat/Huron never accused him of being a drunkard, although Immortal Scoundrel makes much of the insinuation. Champlain may have tried to placate the Roman Catholic Church, or was he jealous? As an explorer in North America, Brûlé accomplished far more than he did. Champlain's wretched little colony at Québec was too feeble to withstand attack by English pirates, and his failed assault on the Iroquois in 1615 was a humiliation for France. In his published journals, Champlain seems to make a point of not naming Brûlé, and it's possible he appropriated Brûlé's maps and incorporated them into his own. A map indicating a southern part of the route Brûlé and the 12 warriors took from Lake Simcoe in 1615 suggests they followed a path west of the Toronto Carrying Place and crossed Lake Erie. There is no evidence that Brûlé was ritually tortured and eaten.

IV: THE DEMISE OF THE WENDAT

Since neither the victorious Iroquois, nor the defeated Wendat, Petun and Neutral nations, the latter dispersed after the destruction of Huronia, left oral histories of this traumatic period, the writings of the French, especially *The Jesuit Relations,* were the primary source of information until intensive archaeological work began in the late 19th century. *Huronia: A History and Geography of the Huron Indians 1600 -1650,* by Conrad Heidenreich, McClelland and Stewart, 1971, 337 pp. is a sweeping, scholarly analysis of every aspect of Huron society based on this research, Heidenreich's own expertise as a geographer and his study of cartography.

The Children of Aataentsic, A History of the Huron People to 1660, Vols. 1 and 2, by Bruce G. Trigger, McGill-Queen's University Press, 1976, is eloquent and empathetic towards the Huron. Trigger stresses the disruption and animosity caused by the attitudes of the priests, especially Jean de Brébeuf's combative, adversarial stance towards the shamans. Returning from a trip to the Neutral in March 1641, Brébeuf fell on the ice on Lake Simcoe and broke a shoulder bone; he may have used the Toronto Carrying Place on his homeward journey.

Essential to an appreciation of the vitality and complexity of Wendat/Huron society are two books by language scholar, John Steckley: *Words of the Huron,* Wilfrid Laurier University Press, 2007, 259 pp. and his translation into English of Gabriel Sagard's *Dictionary of the Huron,* op. cit. Not only is the language complex, but it

This view of Fort Toronto, its harbour and pier was painted in 1839 by Philip John Bainbridge.

emphasizes aspects of life often missing from the archaeological record. Fishing and berry-picking were as important as corn in the annual cycle, and rush mats were used for sitting, sleeping and making sacred bundles. Steckley identifies the burbot, a freshwater cod, as the smelly fish the Wendat dried whole, then boiled with their cornmeal, a healthy source of cod liver oil.

V: The Search for the China Sea

Hennepin's quote comes from *A New Discovery of a Vast Country in America,* by Father Louis Hennepin, Chicago, A.C. McClurg & Co., 1903, vol. 1. Hennepin's vivid memoir was first published in French in 1697. His melodramatic journalism made him a celebrity, and the centre of controversy: Hennepin claimed that during the month of March 1680, he had descended the Mississippi River to its mouth, and returned to its headwaters where he was captured by the Sioux [Dakota]. He, therefore, not La Salle, deserved the credit. Since Hennepin had informed no one of this almost impossible feat during La Salle's lifetime, or his own residence in New France, his story was dismissed as a hoax. *The Dictionary of Canadian Biography* portrays Hennepin as an abrasive man with a talent for making enemies wherever he went.

La Salle and the Discovery of the Great West: France and England in North America, by Francis Parkman, Boston, Little, Brown, & Company, 1931, first published in the late 19th century, remains the only comprehensive biography. The passages describing La Salle's trips on the Toronto Carrying Place come from *Lettres de Cavelier de La Salle et correspondance relative à ses enterprises, 1678-1685,* compiled and edited by Pierre Margry, Paris, Maisonneuve et Cie. This English translation is by Irene Krispis, Toronto. Many of the accounts of La Salle's voyages are of dubious authenticity.

Count Frontenac and New France under Louis XIV, by Francis Parkman, Toronto, George Morang & Co. 1901. Originally published in 1877, this companion volume to Parkman's biography of La Salle portrays the social and political background that places La Salle's actions in context. W.J. Eccles' essay, "Buade de Frontenac," in the DCB outlines the intrigues that helped create chaos in New France.

VI: Turbulent Times

The Ojibwa of Southern Ontario, by Peter S. Schmalz, University of Toronto Press, 1991, uses 17th-century French sources and Ojibwe oral history, recorded in English in the 19th century, to tell how the Algonquins massacred Iroquois war parties in three violent battles on Lake Huron between 1653 and 1662 and drove them south of Nottawasaga Bay: "Nottaway" is one Algonquin spelling for "Iroquois". Schmalz also emphasizes that many of the English traders were as drunk, or drunker, than their customers. He quotes

semi-literate Toronto trader Ferrall Wade complaining about his alcoholic partner: "He does not know what we are about, or the price of a single knife on the Whole he is One of the Most Lazy, Indolent Young fellows I ever saw, the whole Winter he sate by the fire side with his Elbow on his knee & his Chin on his hand picking his nose without speaking a Word he has wore a shirt 13 or 14 weeks without Changing & the Whole time I don't think he Ever Washed, when he took his shirt Off ... it was swarmed with lice." (pp. 68-69)

The excerpts are from Alexander Henry's *Travels and Adventures in Canada and the Indian territories between the years 1760 and 1776,* New York, 1809. Henry had many more adventures during his long life. Setting up as a merchant in Montreal, he continued to trade at Michilimackinac and on Lake Superior; in 1775, he and a few Montreal colleagues ventured into the Northwest as far as the Saskatchewan and Churchill Rivers, challenging the Hudson's Bay Company's fur trade monopoly. Briefly a partner in the North West Company, Henry was a founder of the Beaver Club, a captain in the militia and a justice of the peace. Henry seems to have lost as many fortunes as he made – he had to work as an auctioneer in his old age – but he was highly regarded by his host of influential friends. He died in 1824 at age 85. He wrote only one book, but his *Travels and Adventures* is a classic of Canadian literature.

The Conspiracy of Pontiac and the Indian War after the Conquest of Canada, by Francis Parkman, Toronto, George Morang & Company, 1907 is marred by Parkman's antiquated, 19th-century attitude towards the "savage" or "red man", but he does not demonize Pontiac and attempts to bring some coherence to a tumultuous period in Great Lakes history. Schmalz's *The Ojibwa of Southern Ontario* gives a much more balanced and complex picture of the conflicts among the Algonquin nations and their various motives. He argues that they did not see Pontiac's eventual retreat as surrender; Sir William Johnson bought the peace with lavish gifts and false promises of prosperity and friendship.

La Société d'histoire de Toronto has the William Daniels study, "Locating the Rousseaux Home-Site," op. cit. and a thesis, "Jean-Baptiste Rousseau: Toronto's First Shopkeeper," by Sylvie Beaudreau, York University, 1988.

"Mr. St. John" may have been a play on "St. John the Baptist," or it is possible the Humber River was known as "St. John's" long before Rousseaux settled there?

Percy Robinson's *Toronto During the French Regime,* op. cit. has an extensive history of the first French trading posts. *Landmarks of Toronto: a collection of historical sketches of the old town of York from 1792 until 1833 and of Toronto from 1834 to [1914],* by John Ross

Robertson, published by his newspaper, the *Toronto Evening Telegram,* has a long essay on "The Old French Fort", Fort Rouillé, including the quote from Father Piquet and the incident of the supposed raid on it by the Mississauga.

VII: JOHN GRAVES SIMCOE
BOOKS:

The Correspondence of Lieut. Governor John Graves Simcoe, with Allied Documents, 5 vol. ed. E.A. Cruikshank, Ontario Historical Society. A letter from Simcoe to a British official in Vol. 2, p. 70, indicates that he built the King's Mill by scavenging from an earlier mill: "I have been able to make out from the Iron works of an Old mill that has been permitted to go to ruin sufficient to complete one saw, instead of a Gang of saws." This mill must have been built by the French.

Alexander Macdonnell's personal diary is in Vol. 2, pp. 70-79. Pilkington's map is included. Simcoe seems to have kept no official diary of the expedition. Surveyor Aitken's diary is in the office of the Surveyor-General, Ontario Department of Natural Resources, Peterborough, ON. FNB Vol. 1, pp. 251-254. Controversy surrounds Macdonnell's reference to the "red pine fort" and the exact location of the landing place; the consensus is that it is a short distance north of the end of Yonge St. at Doane Rd. in East Gwillimbury. The sloping promontory, privately owned, has been largely preserved in its natural state. Since it was frequented by the Algonquin travelling to and from Lake Ontario, the "fort" may have been a trading post, or possibly an earlier British survey party had built a shelter. In *Men and Meridians: A History of Surveying and Mapping in Canada,* Don Thompson argues that Samuel Holland was too old and infirm to have surveyed the river himself. Holland had been a friend of Simcoe's father.

The Life and Times of General John Graves Simcoe, D.B. Read, Toronto, Virtue, 1890.

The Life of John Graves Simcoe, W.R. Riddell, McClelland & Stewart, Toronto.

The Town of York, 1793-1815, Edith Firth, Champlain Society, Toronto.

The Diary of Mrs. John Graves Simcoe; notes and biography by John Ross Robertson, op.cit.

Mrs. Simcoe's Diary, ed. Mary Quayle Innis, Macmillan, 1965, 221 pp. Simcoe's correspondence reveals that he aggressively promoted himself and his ideas, and while his utopian vision of creating an Upper Canadian capital, London, in a remote, inaccessible forest, was unrealistic and impractical, he clung to it stubbornly. Horrified by the prospect that the war between the United States and the Western First Nations would spill north into Upper Canada as the "long knives", the U.S. Army, invaded the Ohio Valley, Simcoe advocated British "factories," or trading posts on the upper Mississippi River, and development of the overland route to the Pacific Ocean discovered by Sir Alexander Mackenzie. Only the second came to fruition, via the Canadian Pacific Railway, nearly a century later. Simcoe had an exaggerated opinion of York's virtues as a fortress, and too much faith in unscrupulous colonization schemes. As Richard Cartwright, a critical member of the Legislative Council complained, Simcoe wanted to accomplish in two to three years the work of a century. It must have hurt Simcoe's pride, as well as his social standing, that he had not received the common courtesy of a knighthood on his appointment, and had been refused promotion from lieutenant-colonel to major-general, yet he refused to be subservient to Canada's governor, Lord Dorchester, and expressed his opposition forcefully. It was more than coincidence that Simcoe left Canada the summer the British finally surrendered Forts Niagara, Detroit and Michilimackinac to the United States.

Elizabeth Simcoe wept uncontrollably the day they left York for England, July 21, 1796; she does not tell us her husband's feelings, except to report that he was unwell, and so fearful of the heat and mosquitoes they dined outdoors and, soaked with spray from the rapids, slept in their open bateau during their 10-day trip down the St. Lawrence. Yet, within months of reaching England, Simcoe accepted an appointment as commander of San Domingo, an island in the West Indies notorious for yellow fever. He survived his brief tenure. Then, in 1806, apparently bored with life as a country gentleman and commander of the Plymouth garrison, he was appointed commander of the British forces in India. At sea, he became so ill the ship returned to England; Simcoe died at Exeter on October 26, 1806.

Elizabeth survived her husband by 44 years. Described as autocratic and proud, she did not remarry, and did not permit her six daughters to marry. Her beloved son Francis was killed in battle in 1812, age 22.

Jean-Baptiste Rousseaux established a grist mill, store and inn that served the Ancaster area. In 1797, he purchased 94,000 acres of Six Nations land and sold it the next year to a British partner; the legality of Joseph Brant's land sales is still being challenged. A lieutenant colonel in the York militia, Rousseaux died of pleurisy in 1812 shortly after participating in the Battle of Queenston Heights.

THE TORONTO PURCHASE:
BOOKS
The most authoritative source on the Mississauga Land Claim is a straightforward, 42-page report prepared by the Canadian government's Indian Claims Commission: www.indianclaims.ca/pdf/mississauga.

The Ojibwa of Southern Ontario, Peter S. Schmalz, op. cit.

Sacred Feathers: The Reverend Peter Jones (Kahkewaquonaby) and the Mississauga Indians, Donald B. Smith, U of T Press, 1987.

"The Toronto Purchase," Appendix to the second edition (1965) of Percy Robinson's *Toronto During the French Régime.* Op. cit.

The Town of York, 1793-1815, by Edith Firth (op. cit.) pp. 84-85, gives the Crown's statement of the case against Charles McCuen [McEwan] for the murder of Waipykanine on August 20, 1796. Four witnesses, all British, agreed that McCuen had knocked Waipykanine down, but that McCuen was demanding a dollar from him, not offering it to his sister. The assault on Waipkanine's wife is not mentioned, and two of the witnesses claimed to have seen Waipykanine alive at the Credit River two days later.

VIII: Dreams of England on the Humber
BOOKS
Early Life in Upper Canada, Edwin C. Guillet, Toronto, Ontario Publishing Co., 1933. 782 pp. 318 illus. Guillet says the battle of York lasted about eight hours. British casualties were 62 killed, 72 wounded and 250 taken prisoner; the Americans claimed 14 killed and 23 wounded in battle, 132 killed and wounded by the explosion.

Toronto of Old, Henry Scadding, abridged and edited by F.H. Armstrong, Toronto, Oxford University Press, 1966. The complete edition was published in 1873. Scadding writes that the landing place of the invader "was just within the curve of the Humber Bay, where Queen Street now skirts the beach for a short distance and then emerges on it." Other accounts place the landing closer to Fort Rouillé, but Scadding is meticulous about all his locations.

The Merchant-Millers of the Humber Valley, Sidney Thomson Fisher, NC Press, Toronto, 1985. While building their own electronics company in Montreal, Sidney and his twin brother, Charles, collected rare books. In 1973, in recognition of the donation of their collection, especially Folio editions of Shakespeare's plays, the University of Toronto named its new Rare Book Library in honour of their great-grandfather, Thomas Fisher.

A History of Vaughan Township, G. Elmore Reaman, U of T Press, 1971, 346 pp.

Memories of Weston, Vol. 1: Village of Weston, Weston Historical Society, 1981

A Pictorial History of Weston, Weston Historical Society

The Settlement of York County, John Mitchell, County of York, 1952, 114 pp.

The Woodbridge Story, Herb Sawdon. (no publisher listed)

Landmarks of Toronto, John Ross Robertson, op cit. contains a great deal of detail about the mills and their related businesses. John Scarlett's estate, Runnymede, featured a popular racetrack. In 1840, William Cooper sold his mills to a young American immigrant, William Pearce Howland, who changed the name to Lambton Mills. In 1857, Howland began a distinguished career as a Reform member of the Legislative Assembly, a cabinet minister and, in 1867, was a Father of Confederation. The next year, he was appointed Lieutenant-Governor of Ontario and was knighted in 1879. The Lambton House Hotel, the mill's old red brick inn on the east bank of the Humber River at Old Dundas Street, has been restored as a National Historic Site. The district is still known as Lambton.

James Baby, a member of an old and wealthy Quebec family, had studied fencing and dancing in his youth, and on a grand tour of Europe he had eloped with an actress; he was recalled to Quebec, and the bride paid off. James likely owed his preferment to Elizabeth Simcoe's warm friendship with Marie-Anne Baby, wife of his uncle François. Nearly 40 years younger than her husband, Marie-Anne was 20 in 1791 when the Simcoes spent their first winter in Quebec. Elizabeth Simcoe was 25. Dinners and excursions with "Madame Báby" are frequently recorded in Mrs. Simcoe's diary.

IX: The War of 1812
BOOKS;
Through Water, Ice and Fire: Schooner Nancy of the War of 1812, Barry Gough, Dundurn Group, Toronto, 2006, 213 p. Lively and well-researched, Gough's history includes Commodore Sinclair's Report (Appendix B), McDouall's Report on Worsley's War (Appendix C), and Robert Livingston's petition (Appendix D.)
The Invasion of Canada, 1812-1813, and *Flames Across the Border, 1813-1814,* by Pierre Berton, McClelland & Stewart, Toronto, 1981, each 492 pp.

A History of Simcoe County, Andrew F Hunter, Historical Commission of Simcoe County, 1909.

The Yonge Street Story, 1793-1860, F.R. Berchem, Natural Heritage/Natural History Inc., 1996, 192 pp.

PAMPHLETS:
"Fort Willow and the Nine Mine Portage," Keith H.J. Bacon, Fort Willow Improvement Group, 2000. Authoritative overview with illustrations and a map of the portage based on an 1820 survey. At first, the depot was known simply as "Nottawasaga."

"HMS Nancy: The Legacy of a War of 1812 Schooner and her Crew," Friends of Nancy Island & Wasaga Beach Park. As the years passed, the remains of the Nancy's hull, buried in sand and silt, formed an island in the river. In 1927, it was excavated to form the centrepiece of a museum, now the Nancy Island Historic Site. In spite of the parking lots, billboards and sunbathers, it is still possible to stand on Wasaga Beach on an August morning and imagine the billowing sails of the American warships sweeping down the bay.

DOCUMENTS: Simcoe County Archives, Minesing, Ontario

"An Autobiographical Sketch of the Services of the Late Captain Andrew Bulger of the Royal Newfoundland Fencible Regiment," Bangalore, 1865, pp. 8-15. Norman D. Clarke Papers, Acc. No. 979-38.

"Copy of Lieut. M. Worsley's Letter from America," Jane Simpson Papers, Acc. Museum, 1966.

"The Nine-Mile Portage from Kempenfeldt Bay to the Nottawasaga River," Wilfrid Jury and Elsie Mcleod Jury, Museum Bulletin no.11, Museum of Indian Archaeology, University of Western Ontario, London, ON, 1956.

Recent artists' drawings portray the depot as a much more elegant and permanent establishment than it probably was. No battles were fought there.

Note: On Highway 26 near Edendale a stone cairn with a bronze plaque commemorates the "Glengarry Landing". The inscription reads: "At the forks of the Nottawasaga River, Lt.-Col. Robert McDouall, Glengarry Light Infantry, built the flotilla of boats with which he effected the relief of the British garrison at Fort Michilimackinac …" There is a strong local tradition that McDouall's bateaux were built at the confluence of the Nottawasaga and Marl Creek, several miles downstream from Fort Willow, a place that came to be called Glengarry Landing. The cairn, erected in 1936, is now a National Historic Site, but according to Fort Willow historian Keith H.J. Bacon, any documentation regarding Glengarry Landing has been lost, and it has never been investigated by archaeologists. In the depths of the swamp, it was nowhere near the 9 Mile Portage, or any other major trail, and the Nottawasaga has numerous forks. Commander McDouall was the only member of the Glengarry regiment on the expedition. The historical evidence points to Fort Willow and Willow Creek as the site of the original bateaux construction. (See Simcoe County Archives: council minutes and newspaper clippings re theJ96 1938 unveiling of the cairn.)

FORT WILLOW SIDEBAR:
BOOKS:
Lord Selkirk of Red River, John Morgan Gray, Macmillan, Toronto, 1963. 388 pp.

Governor Simcoe Slept Here: The Legacy of West Gwillimbury, Bradford West Gwillimbury Local History Association.

The Shoe and Canoe, John. J. Bigsby, Paladin Press, New York, Vol. II.

Narrative of A Second Expedition to the Shores of the Polar Sea, in the years 1825, 1826 and 1827, John Franklin, M.G. Hurtig reprint, Edmonton. Introduction, pp xxxi-xxxii.

ARCHIVES:
David Thompson's letters, 1817-1827, are in the Thomas Barclay Collection (26), Maine Historical Society, Portland, Maine. Available online at: http://mainehistory.pastperfect-online.com. *Thompson's Narrative,* published in several editions by the Champlain Society, is a self-portrait of an extraordinary man.

Simcoe County Archives has "Memories of a Pioneer," by Rev. Thomas Williams, published in *Simcoe Country Pioneer Papers,* Mika Publishing, Belleville, ON, 1974. Originally published in 1908, Williams' memoir seems to be responsible for the myth – "old sailor yarns" he calls it – that some 15 to 20 Glengarry Fencibles helped to defend the schooner Nancy in 1814, and covered the British retreat upriver by felling trees and lying in ambush for the pursuing Americans. Williams says: "About dusk they came along and got entangled in the branches of the fallen trees … the guard, who had gathered every musket of the party to the one spot, taking deliberate aim, gave them a deadly volley, and another, and another." Williams calls the repulsion of the Yankees the "Glengarry Fight" at "Glengarry Camp".

An early plan of the City of Toronto, 1857, by lithographer J. Ellis,
originally published by Fleming, Rideout and Schreiber

X: Transforming Ontario

The Weston Historical Society's illustrated publications include *Souvenir of Weston*, 1907.

My biography of geologist-explorer Joseph Burr Tyrrell, *Measuring Mother Earth: How Joe the Kid Became Tyrrell of the North,* covers Joe's early years in Weston; his father, William, was the village's first reeve, his grandfather was Rowland Burr. *The Woodbridge Story,* op.cit. has a brief biography of Burr. "The long forgotten proposal to build a 'Ship Canal' through King Township," by Robert Hulley, *Tapestry* magazine, Fall, 2009, includes a map.

William Lyon Mackenzie's quote is from *The Life and Times of William Lyon Mackenzie,* by Charles Lindsey, Toronto, 1862. Vol. II.

The Firebrand, by William Kilbourn, Clarke, Irwin & Company, Toronto, 1956, is more objective.

The Humber: Tales of a Canadian Heritage River, by Ron Fletcher, RWF Heritage Publication, Toronto, 2006. Pen portraits of many of the colourful characters and events including Robert Home Smith and Conn Smythe; early photographs.

Conn Smythe: If You Can't Beat'Em in the Alley, with Scott Young, McClelland & Stewart, 1981.

"The Archaeology and History of Teiaiagon, Baby Point, City of Toronto, Ontario," a background research report prepared for the City of Toronto by Archaeological Services Inc. in 2005 is brief but informative. Ronald F. Williamson and Annie Veilleux analyze the antler comb in "A Review of Northern Iroquoian Decorated Bone and Antler Artifacts: A Search for Meaning," Ontario Archaeology, No. 79/80.

"The Marsh Story" in *Governor Simcoe Slept Here,* gives a detailed account of the drainage scheme, including the excerpt from the Newmarket Era. Cynics called it "The Big Scam", a way to unload worthless swamp on naïve immigrants. Residents did without roads, electricity and running water for years because the townships were convinced the project was doomed to fail.

And the Swamp Flourished: The Bittersweet Story of the Holland Marsh, by Albert VanderMey, Vanderheide Publishing Co. Ltd. 1994, www.GoDutch.com. VanderMey, tells the story of the Dutch settlers largely in their own frank and eloquent words, with some 200 photographs, many from family albums. The quotes are on pages 25 and 26. The King Township Archives also has transcripts of tape-recorded interviews with Marsh pioneers.

"The Holland Marsh Agricultural Impact Study," Planscape Inc. 2009.

Personal Communication and Photos: Frank Jonkman, Drainage Superintendant and Project Engineer on the canal relocation and restoration.

XI: Hurricaine Hazel and the Holland Marsh

"The Flood – October 15, 1954: A Survivor Remembers," by Addy Ellens, was published in *The King Township Sentinel,* October 20, 2004, p. 9. Passages quoted with the author's permission. *And the Swamp Flourished* includes stories of the flood.

Hurricane Hazel: Canada's Storm of the Century, by Jim Gifford, The Dundurn Group, 2004. Dramatic photos, personal stories. The Dave Phillips quote is on page 41.

Hurricane Hazel, by Betty Kennedy, Macmillan, Toronto, 1979, is the definitive history. Quotes with permission from the author.

The quote from *Hurricane Hazel: Storm of the Century* was reprinted with permission from Dundurn Press Ltd. Copyright 2004.

"Hurricane Hazel: 50th Anniversary." Heritage York Foundation, 2004. DVD video. Personal Recollections.

The Toronto Region Conservation Authority has a library of scientific studies, task force reports, strategic plans and its own history, *Paths to the Living City,* by Bill McLean, TRCA, 2004, 251 pp.

Listen to Your River, a 2007 report card, gave the Humber River Watershed only a C grade based on 26 indicators of health. In 2008, The Humber River Watershed Plan stressed the preservation and enhancement of forest, wildlife, and natural features in the face of urbanization, a position supported by provincial legislation, the Oak Ridges Moraine Foundation and the Oak Ridges Moraine Land Trust. A 2009 report card by the Lake Simcoe Region Conservation Authority raised serious concerns about high levels of phosphorous in the water and the proliferation of algae and invasive aquatic plants.

EPILOGUE:

"The Toronto Carrying Place Trail Today," by Dr. Shaun J. Austin, 4th draft background report, Humber Watershed Cultural Heritage Study, March 1996.

ANN LOVE

Preceeding page: "Morning Fog",
taken on the Oak Ridges Moraine.

Author Heather Robertson and
modern voyageur Paul Pepperall
on the Nottawasaga River, October
2009. The photograph was taken by
artist and naturalist Ann Love, who
joined them on the river.

AUTHOR and journalist Heather Robertson has more than a dozen books and hundreds of articles to her name. Among them are her 1983 novel, *Willie: A Romance,* which won both the Canadian Authors Association Fiction Prize and the Books in Canada Best First Novel Award, and her 1995 biography, *Driving Force: The McLaughlin Family and the Age of the Car,* which won a National Business Award.

Her 2003 history *Magical, Mysterious Lake of the Woods,* co-authored with the late Melinda McCracken and published by Heartland Associates, won the Ontario History Society's Fred Landon Award, presented once every three years for the province's best regional history.

A founding member of both the Writers Union of Canada and the Professional Writers Association of Canada, Heather served as the class representative in Robertson vs. Thomson, a successful class action lawsuit over electronic rights for freelance writers.

A native of Winnipeg, Heather has lived for many years in King City, on the Oak Ridges Moraine north of Toronto.